THE ESSENCE OF HORSEMANSHIP

Dedicated to the German Association of Judges

on the occasion of its 10th Jubilee

and to its most distinguished first president

Major General A. D. Horst-Niemack

Waldemar Seunig

THE ESSENCE OF HORSEMANSHIP

FROM PRACTICAL EXPERIENCE
FOR PRACTICAL USAGE
WITH DRAWINGS BY THE AUTHOR

Translated by Jacqueline Stirlin Harris

J. A. Allen
LONDON

First published in the German language
by Erich Hoffmann Verlag, 1961

English translation copyright
© 1983 by
J. A. Allen & Co. Ltd.
1 Lower Grosvenor Place,
London, SW1W 0EL

British Library Cataloguing in Publication Data
Seuig, Waldemar
The essence of horsemanship.
1. Horsemanship
I. Title
798. '2   SF309

ISBN 0-85131-336-1

First English edition published 1983
Reprinted 1986

Printed and bound in Great Britain by
The Garden City Press Limited
Letchworth, Hertfordshire SG6 1JS

Contents

The illustrations in this book were prepared by the author, and out of respect for his work, the publishers have not presumed to interfere with them. Therefore, although some appear unfinished, they are faithfully reproduced in their original state in compliance with the Author's wishes.

Foreword

THIS ELEMENTARY textbook seeks to strike a responsive chord during a period when 'no one has any time' and when many only take time to balance accounts, look at market reports and read menus. It sums up with concise brevity — if not to say in telegraphic style — the measure of ability of the rider and the advice and instruction from teacher to rider during the correct development of a horse.

'The Essence of Horsemanship' is, if you will, the twice times two table of riding, prerequisite to progressing to more advanced stages. It is an illustrated book of the basics of riding unchanged by the passing of time and fashion.

In my books, 'From the Pasture to the Capriole,' 'Riding Instruction Today,' and in the second part of 'Masters of the Equestrian Art and Their Ways,' I dealt in detail with the fundamentals of riding instruction and dressage, as well as with anatomical and psychological conditions and the resulting interplay of the laws of nature. In this particular book, as I have summed it up in the subtitle, 'From practical experience for practical usage,' I have had the courage to eliminate all unnecessary frills; I have knowingly concentrated only upon the logical progression of exercises which are essential to bring along a horse in the schooling arena or in the open, for recreation as well as for dressage. Here are the exercises needed to put the horse correctly on the aids and which will therefore, in the surest way, show the rider the correct and most pleasant way to arrive at his goal.

I hope that this book, through its unique method of presentation, will find favour with today's riders who, as children of these times, do not wish to take the time for academic study but would rather have, above all, practical guidance to achieve their ends. I have adopted the plan of listing likely faults and immediately giving the practical remedy for their correction, avoiding a 'professor's pen;' and in my drawings I give hints that will, hopefully, eliminate some of the errors which a more technical approach might illustrate less effectively.

I have deliberately substituted drawings for photographs. Without wishing to offend the artists of the camera, I have found that, too often, chance plays too big a part; and it is possible, as a well-known rider pointed out in studying some of the photographs of the Grand Prix de Dressage in Rome, for a rider in one and the same illustration to be praised to the skies from one point of view and torn down completely from another, all depending on what one is looking for.

WALDEMAR SEUNIG.

Preface

THE PLEASURE I have had in translating Waldemar Seunig's 'Am Pulsschlag der Reitkunst' was greatly affected by the news of Col. Seunig's death on December 24, 1976, in his 90th year, in Munich. This great author, great rider, great judge and, above all, this great personality will be sorely missed by all of us who were so privileged to have known him.

In this translation, I have attempted to adhere closely to the text and yet, hopefully, transmit it with the clear intention of this outstanding instructor.

It would be impossible to overestimate the value of the assistance and scholarship of Ursula Sommer of Fairleigh Dickinson University. To her my most sincere and most profound thanks, as well as to my husband who, though not a German scholar, greatly assisted in refining the English prose.

I am also greatly indebted to Dr. H. L. M. Van Schaik, distinguished rider, judge, teacher, of Cavendish, Vermont, who 'fine-tuned' the final draft.

In these tributes, I do not seek to evade my responsibility for any omissions in this translation.

JACQUELINE S. HARRIS

PART ONE

WORK ON THE SNAFFLE

A

Development of suppleness
on the aids, from the untrained horse,
by teaching impulsion.

Suppling-up by driving and lateral aids

A 1
The Working Trot

THE HORSE can most successfully and lastingly be made supple through work at the trot. Tempo: About 275 metres per minute, depending on his activity.

Assumption: The young horse must already have reached a state of confidence and be familiar with the natural, regular trot. This means that, after it has worked off its initial tenseness (see A 5., 'Jumping Free,' page 11), it should trot along, unrestrained, without either rushing or being behind the bit, with natural self-carriage on very light rein contact on a straight line.

Purpose: Responding to the driving aids — the increased thrust of the hindquarters — the horse should move forward in regular and increasingly longer strides, coming onto the bit. Through forward, downward extended neck and a marked oscillation of the back, the contact becomes more definite. The neck is stabilized in front of the withers. Preparation has now commenced for the other movements at the trot.

Aids: Once the horse is sufficiently supple (A 5., 'Jumping Free'), it is basic to gradually shorten the reins. The rider remains in a rising trot until the horse's back starts to oscillate. Now, gently, the rider starts to sit the trot and, glued to the saddle, follows its movement back and forth as he lets himself be drawn ever further down. The rider continually tests the independence of his seat and the self-carriage of the horse by running his hand up the horse's neck. The horse must allow himself to 'be driven.' Therefore he must already understand and respond to the driving aids so that he maintains the tempo as determined by the effect of the seat and the regulating hands, neither rushing nor becoming cramped. The gait shall, with a relaxed back and even contact, be lively and rhythmic, in other words, pure.

Error	*Correction*
Uneven strides.	(a) If the cause is the result of hurried work and of asking too much too soon, the tempo must be decreased until the strides of the hind legs become even again.
	(b) If the cause is a result of constraint, drive with the legs.

Error	*Correction*
Dragging strides.	The rider uses his back and legs to bring the hindquarters more actively under the horse and freshen its gait.
The horse does not respond to the invitation to accept the bit. The horse is not fully ready to answer the driving seat and opening hands by stretching his neck thereby remaining on the bit, and actively accepting it.	See A6. 'Turn on the Forehand.'
The hands try to force the horse onto the bit.	Steady, soft hands following the horse's mouth forward. More freedom for the horse. Livelier tempo.
The nose comes behind the vertical, his neck is shortened and arched, with an over-bent poll.	As above. Very slight, only momentary elevation of the hands. Continued elevation of the reins is useless and harmful, as it will only achieve the opposite movement: more pronounced dropping of the horse's head.
Sideward bend of the neck away from the horizontal.	Slightly elevate the rein on the convex side of the horse's neck, placing it against the point of maximum neck bulge. Avoid pulling backwards! (cf., A 7. 'Straightness' page 16).

THE WORKING TROT

Working trot
Horse's mouth at approximate level of point of the hip.

Working trot

As a result of too high carriage and false collection, the hind legs leave the ground too late. The uncollected horse moves with stiff quarters trailing out behind. The co-ordination between hindquarters and forehand is interrupted (there is a curve in the vertical line of the back), and the horse, not evenly on the bit, is a so-called 'stiff mover'.

A 2
Commencing Riding in the Corners
and on a Large Circle

MOST USEFUL is an open arena, 30 by 60 metres; only if such an arena is not available use an enclosed arena of 20 by 40 metres. In any event, flatten the corners so as to make an elipse of the whole riding area.

Do not yet ask for any bending either on the large circle or in the corners.

Purpose: First principles of turning wherein the impulsion of the hind quarters should follow undiminished towards the forehand. Tempo, rhythm and carriage should remain undisturbed, identical to working on a straight line.

Aids: Inside 'opening' rein slightly away from the horse's neck indicates a new direction or a change in the size of the circle. The outside rein still without effect (negative rein). At completion of the turn, the inside hand yields in the direction of the horse's mouth.

Error	*Correction*
The 'opening' (inside) hand pulls backwards.	Inside hand indicating a turn must move away perpendicularly from the horse's neck, with thumb up and elbow remaining at the rider's side.

A 3
Lengthening and Shortening the Gait
at the Working Trot

LENGTHEN THE stride on the long side of the arena and shorten it on the short sides. This exercise should begin only when the horse has achieved a certain self-carriage (under the rider) at the working trot and is able to balance himself under the weight of the rider. Should be done only for short periods of time. When working outdoors in open country, proceed on a straight line, preferably toward the stable, at a rising trot. Take advantage of the natural exuberance of the horse's way of moving.

Purpose: Confirmation of the ability of the horse to balance himself, without losing rhythm in the changes of tempo. The stimulation of the impulsion and exuberance of the horse. The horse's yielding to controlling aids. Preparatory steps for achieving ultimate submission.

Aids: When lengthening the strides gradually increase the driving aids. Frequently ride with reins in one hand. When shortening the stride repeatedly increase the tension of the reins with a deep and engaged seat, but do not yet bring its (the seat's) entire effect to bear.

Errors During Lengthening of Stride	*Correction*
Horse falls apart.	While driving forward steadily, maintain a constant contact of hand, slightly modify the tempo.
Hurried, uneven strides.	Reduce the tempo until the rhythm has been re-established.

Errors During Shortening of Stride	*Correction*
Rider's hand becomes stiff in the halting movement and starts to pull. Horse's head comes behind the vertical.	After the half-halt, give with the hands. Do not forget to drive on.
Horse breaks into canter.	Don't pull up abruptly. With a lowered hand move forwards, try to re-establish the trot.

A 4
The Natural Canter

THIS IS the counterpart of the natural trot (see page 3). Very soon after the initial schooling introduce the horse to this gait, on straight lines, in open country, on a sandy or otherwise smooth and springy ground. Next to 'free' jumping or turns on the forehand, this is the best method by which to eliminate all tenseness and thus make the horse supple and prepare him to move freely on the aids. The canter must not be regarded by the horse as 'special event.'

Purpose: To loosen, to have the horse accept the bit confidently, to awaken his impulsion to encourage suppleness of the back, to keep him fresh, to improve steady contact, to quieten, to educate in relaxation and 'giving,' to accustom the horse to remain on the chosen leg. Achievement of a balanced carriage without seeking to use the reins as a 'fifth leg.'

Aids in open country: Rising trot from a forward seat driving forward evenly with both your legs until the horse breaks into a canter onto the right or left leg of his own choice. (The rider treats with casual indifference any initial racing or dashing forward emanating from lack of balance or temperament.) At this point the reins are relatively short and maintain an elastic, fluid, restraining contact with the horse. Later endeavour to get the horse going forward, graduating from a shortened rein to a long rein, ultimately cantering on a free rein when appropriate, so that the rider has the pleasant feeling that even as he gives his reins he 'holds his horse with his seat' in a constant rhythm of even strides.

Should the horse when in open terrain break into a canter of his own accord, it should be accepted thankfully at this stage of training, bearing in mind that soon he must be driven into it!

Aids in the arena: On the circle, moving towards the wall, drive the horse on in the trot until he breaks into the canter. Training whip on the inside shoulder and don't forget to use the voice 'canter' so that only the horse can hear. These are all aids which later can be dropped and replaced by the aids of the inside leg and the inside rein.

To assure that the horse will break into the correct canter lead, the rider must for the time being and against all normal rules rise when the inside front leg and the outside hind leg comes to the ground. This is the only time when rising on this diagonal is permitted.

After several rounds on the circle, enlarge to the whole arena with flattened corners. This exercise should be done only for brief periods of time!

Error	*Correction*
The horse takes the wrong lead on the circle.	Re-establish unconstrained, relaxed trot. Now, again, as described above, break into a canter from trot, rising when the inside front leg and the outside hind leg come to the ground.
Horse rushes on the circle.	Wait until horse goes quietly on large circle, then enlarge to the full arena.
Horse changes lead unasked in the riding school or in the open.	Quieter, closer, more following, evenly distributed neutral seat of the rider. Hands soft, steady and deep.
Rider bounces in the saddle.	The taut small of the back from hips to knees pushed to the front. Knees and heels deep, knee joint and ankle joint elastic.
Rider's hands too high.	Low, passive hand with the small fingers stroking the crest of the neck of the horse under the mane.
Rider's inside hip caves in.	Push inside seat bone forward, inside knee deeper.
Rider's outside shoulder falls to the rear.	Move outside shoulder forward.
Rider looks down to the inside.	Turn head to the outside.
Rider pulls with inside hand.	Inside hand farther forward, then again establish light contact.

A 5
Jumping Free

JUMPING ON the lunge should be an introductory exercise to each riding lesson.

Purpose: Primarily to loosen the back and with that the whole musculature of the horse. Promotion of flexibility. In addition it is educational and helps to quieten the horse. Preparation for jumping with rider. An excellent means to spare the rider a part of the loosening-up work therefore a timesaver.

Aids: Advance from the early leading the horse at a walk over poles lying on the ground, to trotting him on the lunge over a series of cavaletti to cantering over solid and simple obstacles up to the height of 1.10 metres.

After the horse has adopted as second nature the arching of his back and extension of his neck — bascule — while going over cavaletti, lead him from the outside in a free walk up to an obstacle. Open your hand as soon as the horse shows an inclination to jump. A helper places himself with a whip on the near side of the obstacle inside the circle; he must use the whip only very sparingly. If the horse hesitates or attempts to run out, usually only a warning raising of the whip from sideways-backwards is sufficient.

Error	*Correction*
Impetuousness coming up to the obstacle.	The trainer remains behind the shoulder of the horse and works to keep the horse next to him with the reins, mainly the outside rein. He will hold his free hand in front of horse's face and speak soothingly. Straighten the horse repeatedly. Lead the horse in a small circle — trainer on the inside — until composure is regained.
Horse runs out.	Assistant raises his arm sideways. The trainer does not ask the horse to jump until closer to the obstacle. Consider lowering obstacle.
Horse refuses.	Lead horse up again. Possibly lower obstacle.
Horse approaches obstacle hesitatingly.	Lower obstacle. Add take-off bar in front of obstacle.

Error	*Correction*
Horse lands will all four feet simultaneously. (Jumps with stiff back.)	Add take-off bar. Assistant drives horse with whip. More work on the caveletti.

A 6
Turns on the Forehand

FOLLOWING THE principle that the horse should always be physically developed, we start now with turns on the forehand, once the contact at the working trot has become established. This exercise is done at the halt only for as long as it is necessary for the horse to learn to respond to the lateral aids — inside leg, inside rein — and move against the outside leg and outside rein. Then we replace this turn on the forehand from the halt with the turn on the forehand in motion. The forehand now, as a result of the driving influence of the rider's outside leg (the inner leg is concerned with the sideways movement of the horse) will describe a small, concentric or volte-like circle. The hind quarters describe a larger and eccentric circle.

Purpose: The horse is being taught to feel and accept the bit, ultimately to champ and seek it. Commencing of a slight bending along the whole back. The horse learns about the outside aids, to respect them, and respond to them. Preparation for tighter turns; for leg-yielding, without the unfortunate drawbacks associated with the latter; and preparation for work on two-tracks. A good means of bringing the disobedient horse onto the aids. Next to the working trot and free jumping, the best suppling exercise.

Aids: Put horse on the bit. Let the horse champ the bit. Pick up inside rein, require a very slight turn of the entire neck to the inside. Rider's inside leg behind girth presses synchronously with the inside hind foot of the horse as it describes a circle (two hind steps to one) around the forehand. Rider's outside leg insures that the forward movement is contained in short strides and prevents escape from the inside leg by taking up every second stride, so that each time there is a shorter or longer pause between strides, as determined by the rider. The crest of the neck slightly bends to the inside.

Inside rein supports the inside leg; the outside rein is used when necessary as a counterforce should the outside shoulder fall away. The rider's small of the back and legs see to it that both during and after the turn the horse remains on the bit and moving forward. During the turn, the horse must not lose his straightness: his shoulder must remain directly ahead of his hind quarters.

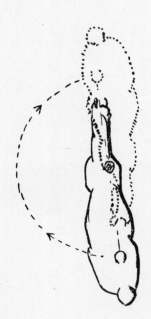

Turn on the forehand
Turn on the forehand
to the right (only a
schooling exercise).

Errors	Correction
Horse does not champ or accept the bit, does not 'give his mouth' to the hands. The readiness to answer the rider's demands for supple responsiveness is absent.	The horse, set with a very slight bending of the neck, but otherwise straight for the time being, is pushed by, e.g., the rider's right leg to move to the left, in even steps. The rider's right hand is raised with a stretched elbow out of the shoulder to near the horse's ears; and, without exercising any pressure, maintains a light contact with the horse's mouth. At this point, thus, the right rein is vertical to the ground. The left hand remains in its normal position, with the fourth and fifth fingers vibrating, opening and closing. The stimulation worked upon the right side of the mouth, will result in a chewing and resultant swallowing. At the moment this occurs the right hand instantly comes down to its normal position. Move out of the circle and ride straight ahead. Drop reins and praise. In logical fashion perform this exercise to both sides. The horse will quickly understand. Soon, leg pressure and an almost imperceptible lifting of the rein will produce chewing and loosening of the horse's mouth even on a straight line.
Horse falls on the outside shoulder. The neck is loose in front of the withers.	Inside hand lighter. Outside rein prevents falling out and keeps neck straight. Possibly omit the slight bend in the neck and for the time being let the horse remain straight during the turn. Possibility of even a 'counter-position.'
Horse resists and tries to evade the bit.	Energetically, by bracing the small of the back and with legs, drive horse several steps straight forward. If necessary, use whip.
Horse stiffens, because it stops moving the front legs.	As above.
Falling away of the outside hind leg which steps too far to the side.	Strengthen outside aids.
Horse tilts the poll. One ear is lower (a salivary gland is pinched by the edge of the jawbone.)	Return to straight work at the working trot (see page 3) until either both glands come under the jaw bones or until both glands appear evenly between the jawbone edges and the neck joint. Now the horse will go evenly on both reins and the ears will be at the same height.

Straightening − Crookedness

GUSTAV STEINBRECHT, to whom the riding art owes so much, gave the following basic advice: 'Ride your horse forward and keep him straight.'

A horse is straight − or square − when his hind legs move close together with impulsion toward the centre of gravity (in the direction of the movement) and when his fore legs and hind legs bear an equal distribution of weight. Therefore, except on the circle and during changes of direction, the inside and outside hind legs must always each support exactly half the effort required of the hindquarters in any movement.

For the horse to *be* square (or straight), as opposed to his moving on a straight line, it is immaterial whether he is bending or not, going on a curve or going on a straight line, whether going on a single or double track; whether free or collected − in this context there is no relationship to or application of a purely formal geometric shape or static line of or to the horse's back or longitudinal axis.*

Straightness is lost as soon as the horse, because of wrong distribution of the rider's weight and equally incorrect rein aids, assumes a false or forced bend, thus becomes crooked or uneven.

Unevenness will result in resistance, in one-sided stiffness of the neck, uneven contact, impure gaits and ultimately lameness.

The so-called 'natural onesidedness' makes itself manifest if the rider begins to force his young untrained horse on to the bit prematurely. Most frequently it will be the right hind foot with which the horse resists, instead of moving straight forward towards the centre of gravity under his body. Therefore, because it moves this leg to the right instead of straight forward it has the tendency to let the diagonal left shoulder fall away and a convex bulging of the neck is the result. The horse moves against the right leg aid and leans against the left rein. The resultant picture is that of a horse in a faulty right travers position.

---

*To avoid misunderstandings, Steinbrecht's interpreters place the term 'straightness' interventionally with 'relative straightness.'

The purpose of these exercises to put the horse straight is to make the horse seek even contact with confidence. This work should already begin during the phase of developing relaxation and suppling, as the natural trot is being stepped up to a working trot and impulsion is developed to the point where the horse adopts a rhythmic, energetic, back-swinging movement, extending his neck, seeking the bit, resulting in an uneven, elastic forward-seeking contact.

Aids: The straightening exercises begin as the horse is placed preparatory to mounting after the free-jumping or lungeing session. Every riding horse, whether a pony or a Thoroughbred, cold or warm blood, should stand squarely on all four legs and quietly on a loose rein as the rider mounts.

Should a horse in the working trot, bear more heavily on one rein than the other, the rider will give with that rein while driving forward so much that the horse must finally take up contact on the heretofore slack rein and stretches and accepts both reins equally.

That the horse's head may frequently turn to the outside as a result of the above, should not disturb the rider. There is an old saying, 'There will be shavings where you plane.' As soon as the horse is even on both reins, the head position will become balanced by itself.

Correction of onesidedness/crookedness by straightening: In order to go to the heart of this matter and to avoid too many theoretical explanations I will give a practical example. It is applicable to both unevenness to the left and to the right and to riding on either hand. For the sake of illustration we will take crookedness from right to left, and the aim is to 'deprive' the horse of support from the right hind foot and the left shoulder.

Lively working trot on the circle to the left. Left rein very loose, for it is the left rein that the horse would like to lean on. Right rein remains soft but with definite contact even at the risk that one has to put up with the wrong head position for a quarter of an hour or more. Left leg slightly behind the girth drives forward and also sideways so as to enlarge the circle, thus the horse's right shoulder kept in front of the evading right hind leg, until the horse starts to reach for and lean into the loose outside rein and thereby establishes on his own an even contact.

At this point, change rein through the circle to the right and the right hind leg now becomes the inside leg, and one attempts to maintain the just won evenness, straightness. This can be achieved by placing the right fore leg in front of the right hind leg by means of both hands rhythmically pushing the shoulders to the inside.

To avoid unevenness or crookedness arising during later training, it is of great value to practise turns on the forehand in motion (volte 'in

17

travers'). The sensitivity and responsiveness to the lateral inside aids must eventually be so well developed that the rider ultimately is able to cause the horse to step around the forehand in motion merely by leading with one hand, pushing forward with his inside hip bone with a shortened inside rein and deep inside knee.

From the exercise, volte 'in travers', (turn on the forehand in motion), the rider will develop leg-yielding.

'Straightness – crookedness'

Horizontal bend
in front of
withers.
Horse is crooked
from right to
left.
Stronger contact
on the left.

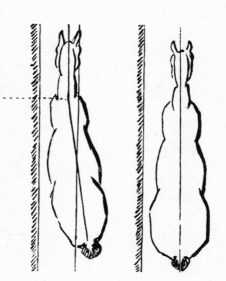

Horse with a
straight spine.
In this particular
case, the horse is
also 'straight' on
a straight line,
which otherwise
exists only in a
text book and in
the imagination
of theoreticians.

Working trot

The diagonal hoof beats are regular, but are dull and dragging. Lack of impulsion and forward reaching of the hind legs, weak hindquarters, poorly connected to rest of body. This should be corrected by a lighter rider, through using a more driving and forward seat, setting the horse's head and neck carriage lower.

Turns on the forehand
'Turn on the forehand to the left in motion and forward march!'
This is the correction for a horse whose dead mouth does not 'give'
and is therefore not champing at the bit.

A 8
Leg Yielding

THE HORSE is still without a longitudinal bend. The horse's head is placed slightly to the inside, therefore against the direction in which he is going. The inside feet pass in front of and over the outside feet.

Execution: At first performed at a shortened walk only for the purpose of showing the horse what is wanted; but essentially to be done only at the working trot since the lesser animation and swing inherent in the walking gait does not supple the horse. Perform this exercise to begin with only on the long sides of the school and on the open side of a circle in the school, and to begin with only on the inside aids. The forehand is brought slightly to the inside of the track. The head position is imperceptibly shortened (this cannot be as yet called a half-halt), and now leg yielding begins. To straighten the horse at the conclusion of the exercise, whether performed on a circle or on a straight line, bring the forehand in front of the hind quarters by pivoting the shoulder around the hind quarters (actually a fractional 'turn on the haunches in motion'). End the exercise shortly before the corner by riding forward with normal straight movement. Always alternate this exercise with repetitive work on a true gait at a lively working trot.

If the horse is to yield to the outside leg — the counter exercise — position the head when the horse's head reaches the second corner of the short side (at the beginning of the long side). Commence the leg yielding in such a way that the hindquarters come out of the corner already on the inside track. End the exercise by resetting the horse's position and resuming the track at the wall in a shallow curve; or even better repositioning the forehand in front of the hindquarters and proceeding in a straight line one stride away from the wall. The rider's leg nearest the wall must prevent the hindquarters from scrambling or staggering back to the outside as is frequently attempted by the horse at this point (an exercise in obedience).

Purpose: To perfect the submission to lateral leg and rein aids. Preparation for two tracks. It is argued that the advantages achieved by this exercise can also be achieved through less 'dangerous' exercises. Following are some of the disadvantages which are often cited:

(a) As the horse is moving only indirectly forward (on three tracks) without being bent, the full development of propulsion and impulsion will be hampered, and there is the threat of loss to correct movement even with a tactful rider.

(b) The hind legs move too much in a sidewise manner and therefore do not carry their share of the weight. The horse which is now scrambling more to the side than moving forwards and sideways loses his carriage and cadence and falls on the shoulder: primarily on the outside shoulder which then is apt to evade to the outside. This falling away is hard to prevent, as it occurs in the direction of the general movement. In addition to this falling away, we must watch for an unwanted loosening of the base of the neck.

(c) In such a crooked movement, in which the forehand does not precede the hindquarters, there is the danger that the inside front legs in crossing over the outside ones are apt to interfere, resulting in splints and similar injuries.

Aids: The aids are briefly tabulated here. (However with the reservations as mentioned above, that we believe leg yielding as a preparation for the half pass could happily be omitted — it is our humble opinion that this exercise, along with the turn on the forehand in place, except as an introduction or correction, are long overdue for a first-class state funeral — and should be replaced to great advantage with more specifically purposeful lessons).

Seat is placed to the inside and forward. The rider's inside leg behind the girth drives to the side in rhythm with the lifting of the horse's inside hind leg. The rider's outside leg drives forward and is ready to control the sideways stepping. The inside rein maintains softness in the poll and the head position which is slightly to the inside. The outside rein contains the shoulder and prevents a tipping of the neck at its base. The outside aids may come into play only when the horse has responded and yielded to those on the inside and therefore moves into the outside aids.

Faults

Most faults will emanate from the circumstances listed under a, b and c above; and they are to be found even among the best riders on well-schooled horses.

Correction

Eliminate leg yielding. Replace with volte 'in travers' (turn on the forehand in motion), and possibly the exercise of contracting and then enlarging the track in the school, which at least is less likely to prevent the horse losing forward movement; then later with serpentines, bending exercises at the walk (first and second position) and, above all, with the exercise of decreasing and increasing the size of the circle at the working trot. Re-establish a true gait by riding the horse forward with even contact on both reins in an energetic working trot on a single track.

23

A 9
Serpentines

ONCE THE horse responds to the inside aids in the turns on the fore-hand, you can begin with serpentines along the long side of the arena.

Start serpentines at a walk only in order to familiarize the horse with the new path he is to follow, but then immediately take up the exercise at a lively working trot. Later on, with a more advanced horse, we will perform the serpentine at a collected trot and finally at a canter. In the latter gait, it can be executed either with or without change of leg. The number of loops is determined by the size of the arena; they should be of even size. For the time being fairly shallow curves will suffice.

As the ability of hindquarters to carry the weight is increased and the horse's ability to collect himself is developed, the loops of the serpentine in a given area can be doubled or tripled.

Execution: It is essential that the horse keeps his hindquarters on the same track as that of his forehand and that transition from loop to loop be executed without hesitation — that is, fluently, without loss of rhythm or tempo.

Aim: Training the horse to be responsive to the turning aids. Development of lateral spinal suppleness in preparation for bending work (first and second position).

Aids: The same as for all turns at any gait on the single, simple, straight forward track. The rider must see to it by change of seat and subtle change of aids, that at each point of the change of direction from loop to loop he keeps the horse on an evenly rounded track and avoids squared corners. The inducement for change of direction should come principally from changes of weight — pushing to the front of the inside seat bone and outside shoulder with an elastically taut back. The changes of weight as an aid fulfil their purpose when they reinforce the turning rein action (which always takes away somewhat from the impulsion and free forward movement of the horse) to the point that only the merest indication of the rein aids will suffice to produce the movement.

The flow of forward movement is best maintained in the natural exuberance of the rising trot, during which the rider's legs with heels down are constantly in light, rhythmic, pulsing contact with the horse's sides. By each seat and leg change especially with the inside knee and heel well down, the horse is driven forward into the next loop. Each time before bending in the new direction, the horse is momentarily put straight. These same principles are also involved in changes through the circle or in riding a figure eight, which at this point, however, do not concern us.

Error	*Correction*
The corners are square rather than round. The horse becomes hesitant and loses his rhythm and tempo.	See aids.

'Walk on a loose rein'
The reins are allowed to hang.

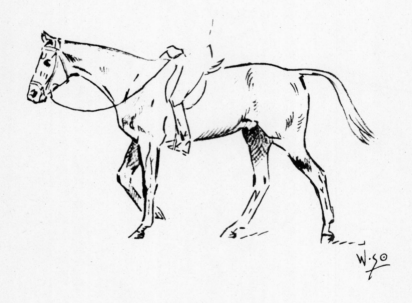

SERPENTINES

**'Work on the circle' and 'riding through
the corners'**

Collected canter to the right. Lateral bending of the spine in the
turn clearly visible. Hind legs brought well under the horse to take
up the weight.

A 10
Work at the Walk I
WALK ON A LONG REIN

UP TO now in all these chapters designated 'A', the walk should be on a completely long rein or on the buckle, as we say. Brief exceptions may be in cases of playfulness or disobedience, as well as appropriate times in the preparation for execution of previously described exercises, and for half-halts which, for the time being, have been merely a shortening or a slowing into a halt.

Aim: To achieve and maintain a free and completely natural walk. To allow the horse to rest the neck muscles tired from the trotting exercises.

Aids: Reins held on the buckle or knotted and laid on the horse's neck. Stimulating legs.

Error	*Correction*
Inexperienced riders: trying to maintain the position of the horse's head during rest periods at the walk damages the gait and will result in tensions and faulty flexion (faulty 'giving in').	Release the reins!

B

Commencing collection by the addition of
impulsion and the outside aids

Transforming the forward drive into 'oscillation'
by means of increased flexion
of the joints* of the hindquarters

Improving the gait at working trot

Medium trot

Working and medium canter

Perfecting lateral flexion of the spine through counter
influence of the outside aids in bending work
('first' and 'second positions') and in turns

Half-halts

Rein back

*Joints can only be flexed but not bent (curved). Therefore, the frequently used expression 'bent hocks,' taken literally would be incorrect

B 1
Work on the Circle

WORK ON the circle is comprised of a fluid series of successive curves and is made possible by the relative lateral bending of the horse's spine. The horse's neck is straight. The inner hind foot keeps in the track of the inner fore foot imprint, the outside hind foot in the direction of the imprint of the outside fore foot. Work on the circle should begin about four to six months after the horse has commenced training. Lively, strong horses might have to start sooner; lethargic horses later. The latter should be worked more frequently in the open with lively, energetic, forward riding.

Aim: To improve the agility and flexibility of the horse in turns by means of increased 'bending' (flexing) of the inside hind leg. Converting the impulsion of the hindquarters to increasing support. Work on the circle is a proven method to turn those strong horses which, with constantly tensed and rigid backs, attempt to rush out from under the rider's seat with short rapid strides, into becoming 'back-swinging movers' with forward and downward extended neck and long rhythmic strides — i.e., to get those horses who only use their legs to also use their backs.

Aids: The seat is forward to the inside; that is to say, the rider pushes forward his inside hip and inside seat bone, with knee and heel down and without altering the outside shoulder; the inside rein controls the turn on the circle and keeps the horse bending inwards and supple. Inside leg is in supple contact slightly behind the girth, working actively to drive forward as soon as the movement starts to lag. As the inside leg is on the horse at the centre of spinal flexion, it is continually ready to maintain this bend through rhythmic pressure in the direction of the outside shoulder. Outside rein controls lateral curve of the spine. It prevents any drifting-out of the shoulder (particularly on the open side of the circle) and supports the leg which is behind the girth on the outside preventing the moving-out of the hindquarters.

A more advanced, schooled horse will be able to maintain these curved lines — serpentines or circles or voltes and all the other bending figures in motion — through the simple balance of weight aids and the corresponding leg position and the correct influence of bringing forward the outside shoulder.

Fault	*Correction*
Liveliness and freedom of working trot are diminished.	Abandon circle. Return to the straight line and in a stronger fresher working trot reawaken the impulsion and forward movement and enthusiasm of the horse.
Hindquarters falling in; false travers position (mostly on the right rein when the inside rein is pulling).	Both legs drive forward. With light contact, re-establish the correct curve, adjusted to the bend of the circle. In general, do not neglect work to keep the horse 'straight' as described in A 7!
Horse's neck becomes loose at the withers. Outside shoulder drifts outward.	Outside rein prevents shoulder from drifting out and straightens the neck firmly in front of the withers so that it maintains the even curve of the spine from the poll to the croup. Essential: Frequent changes of direction.
Horse's hindquarters drift to the outside.	Lighten inside rein. Outside leg and rein act as preventative.
Horse moves away to the outside of the circle.	Turn away from the wall sooner. More outside leg, inside rein. Nevertheless, outside rein must still be used so that the shoulders are positioned properly in front of the hindquarters.
Horse reduces circle of his own accord.	Inside leg applies pressure as in the shoulder-in movement, widening to the outside, supported by the outside rein.
Horse increases size of the circle.	Outside leg applies pressure, as in the travers movement, to the inside with inside rein support. However, outside rein must still see to it that the shoulders remain in correct alignment with the hindquarters.
Rider's inside leg does not hold its position on the rib cage effortlessly, but is pushed away by the horse's movement. The reason for this is that the horse has not yet submitted to and accepted the aids, stiffens himself and does not move along with a true lateral curve of the spine.	First, relaxation and regained calm — (see page 14); only then re-establish the lateral curve of the spine.
Both hands are carried too far to the inside ('neck reining'). Horse's shoulder accordingly drifts to the inside of the circle.	Put horse straight, hands directly in front of your body.
Rider's hip collapses.	Position inside hip forward.
Outside shoulder of the rider hangs back.	By pivoting the hip joint, push the outside shoulder forward.

Fault

Rider pulls on inside rein. If the inside is the 'soft' side, the horse's outside shoulder falls away to the outside, and the hindquarters move inward in a traver-like crooked movement. Should the inside happen to be the 'stiff' side, the hindquarters will drift away to the outside.

The horse rushes and attempts to escape the aids.

Correction

Lighten inside rein.

Any attempt to calm the horse through half-halts will only make him more 'stiff' and therefore make the problem worse. It would be better to use the following correction. Ride a circle which is closed on three sides at the end of the school. Let the horse move ahead at a rising trot. By sitting down into the saddle somewhat against or behind the too rapid movement of the horse slows it and thereby forces the horse to adopt to the rider's slower rising and sitting. However, in spite of all, go along with the horse and for the time being avoid any attempt to regulate the tempo. With sufficient patience the horse will learn to shorten his stride on his own. At that point the flat side of the rider's leg is cautiously placed on the horse's rib cage and remains lightly in this position. The retarding efforts of the rider become more and more frequent. He also, little by little, makes the circle smaller and therefore makes the horse more receptive to a shortened stride. Finally, the rider is able to resume impulsion with driving aids. Once he is able to do this, the hurried action will have stopped; for the hind legs, not striding too short, will begin to try to overcome the difficulty and will make the longer strides necessary for the horse to maintain his position, and he will come back to a slower cadence. The horse regains his self-carriage and will no longer lose his balance in front. The horse accepts the aids which he was evading earlier.

B 2
Half-Halts

HALF-HALTS produce either greater collection or a shortening of tempo, depending on the rider's proportionate emphasis on driving or restraining aids. The quality of the half-halt will determine the quality of the movements to follow.

Aim: Improving rhythm and carriage and thereby, submission to the aids and collection. Lightening the contact in the event that it has become too heavy and the horse leans on the bit. Introduction to and preparation for exercises such as two-track work, canter departs, changes of direction. (While in such instances the half-halt can result in a decreasing of speed or reduction of tempo, these might *not* occur. Riding exercises!) A remedy for rushing. Transition to a slower tempo or lesser gait.

Aids: Tightening of lower back muscles with seat well down and forward in the saddle. A vertical stretching of upper body, above the waist. Knee and heel down. Alternately resisting, then following rein effect with simultaneous passive or activating lateral leg pressure in rhythm with the impulsion of the horse. In contrast to the full-halt, the driving aids overcome and outlast the restraining aids, and the hand allows the forward movement to continue. Horse must flex its neck (relatively) and start to champ the bit. Poll the highest point. In a more advanced, trained horse, it will eventually be sufficient for the rider to tighten his seat and close his fingers to achieve the same effect.

Error	*Correction*
The horse does not wait for the restraining aid. It anticipates the movement and comes behind the bit. Horse arches the neck falsely and his nose comes behind the vertical. Because of the incorrect bend in the neck, the position of the horse's neck is false. The horse is no longer on the bit.	At a lively working trot, bring the horse to the driving aids and lengthening its neck so that he accepts the bit again. Then, with very soft hands, repeat the half-halt.
The rein effect is too harsh (those tiresome 'heavy hands'). The hindquar-	Drive forward; only then take up on the reins.

Error	*Correction*
ters become disunited and fall away to the rear.	
The rider does not give with his hands in response to the forward movement of the horse's head.	Follow more to the front with the hands.

'Riding through the corner'
on correct track

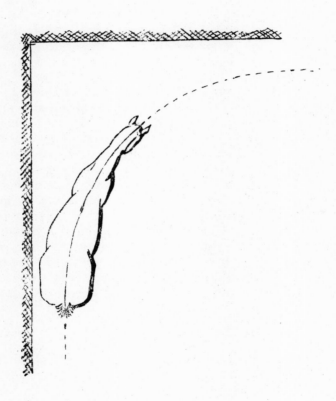

Turns in Motion

(a) RIDING THROUGH THE CORNERS

FIRST STAGE of development: Ride shallow curves, as in serpentine described on page 24. Ride the short side of the riding school as a half circle. Carry weight to the inside. Inside hand remains steady or indicates the turn by lateral leading movement of the hands toward the inside of the curve. The outside rein at first remains passive — completely loose; later yielding. Both legs and whip drive forward.

Second stage: Perform bend with the horse's spine curved on a quarter volte having a radius of three metres. This should only be asked for when a true lateral bend on a volte with a diameter of six metres has been achieved through practice at the collected trot and canter.

Aim: The achievement of a greater degree of fluidity through collection and soft acceptance of and submission to the aids.

Aids: Six strides from the corner half-halt, maintaining the same tempo especially with the assistance of the outside rein. The rider's seat is forward to the inside. Outside shoulder well forward. Inside rein positions the horse and indicates the new direction. Outside rein remains securely in position and together with the outside leg controls the bend of the horse's spine around the inside leg. Both legs (primarily the inside one, because the outside one is passively occupied) maintain the regular forward motion without loss of tempo. Having achieved the new direction, ease the inside rein.

Error	*Correction*
Horse resists correct movement through the corner.	Be sure to put the horse on the aids before the corner. Then, with shortened stride, the aids are applied consecutively leading the horse stride by stride through the turn. General Decarpentry refers to this exercise in the following descriptive words: 'Décomposer les resistances' — the individual resistances separately corrected.
The horse resists during the turn.	See 'Aids'.
The horse hurries through the corner; thus loss of rhythm.	The half-halt before reaching the corner must be more effective.

Error	*Correction*
Drifting outwards of the outside shoulder (particularly on the right hand).	More control with outside rein; inside rein lighter.
Falling away and outwards of the outside hind leg (particularly when riding to the left).	Lighten rein contact on the inside. Preventative action with outside rein and leg.
Out in the open where there are no boundaries, the horse attempts before turning, to evade to the outside therefore avoiding the uncomfortable lateral curving of his body. The track resulting from such a turn becomes too like an 'S' and we have unwanted serpentines.	Preventative action with outside rein and leg.
Faulty bending of the spine (primarily on the left turn).	Inside leg presses into the rib cage. The outside leg prevents the hindquarters falling out and thereby insures the lateral bend of the horse's spine around the inside leg.
The horse straightens the curve against the rider's will.	Stronger influence of the rider's inside leg, immediately behind the girth pressing sideways to the outside, whereby the shoulders are pushed to the outside and the lateral curve or bend of the spine thus resulting permits the riding of a turn with a radius of three metres. Outside rein controls, the inside leg supports outwards and sideways.
The rider guides the horse too far into the corner, then without the counter-action of the inside rein pushes the forehand to the inside with outside hand 'over the withers'.	Do not go so deep into the corner. Inside hand maintains the curve in contact with the horse's mouth. Outside rein controls more lightly.
The rider guides the horse too far into the corner with the inside hand pressing 'over the neck' to the outside.	Into the corner with the outside rein, and *out* of corner with the inside rein.
Both hands of the rider are too far to the inside. Therefore, the inside shoulder leans in during the bend.	Keep the hands in front of the body.
Inside hand pulls into the turn or corner without support from the outside rein; therefore, the hindquarters often fall away to the outside (generally when moving to the left) or to the inside (generally when moving to the right). See corresponding correction under 'Work on the Circle', page 30.	Lighten the inside rein and support with the outside rein.

(b) VOLTES

The volte is a circle with a diameter of six metres; it demands the maximum lateral bending of the horse's spine which can or should be achieved with the horse while tracking correctly (see page 16).

A very instructive exercise to test your control is to ride several voltes one after the other, with a single track or set of hoof prints. (Easily observed in new snow.) This is a polished exercise of which only an expert on a reliable and well-trained horse is capable.

Aim and Aids: See 'Riding Through the Corners' page 36.

Error	*Correction*
Horse rushes during the volte and therefore loses rhythm.	The half-halt before commencing the volte must be more effective. Any correction applied during the volte itself will be too late.
Rider attempts a volte of too small diameter with the result that hindquarters no longer follow in track of the forehand, but fall away to the outside.	With both reins, move the forehand a little to the outside in front of the drifting hindquarters (shoulder leading). The outside leg prevents the hindquarters from moving out any further.

(c) HALF CIRCLE AND CHANGE (OF DIRECTION)

The first half of the movement resembles a half-volte. Then the horse is ridden diagonally back towards the original track. On reaching the track the change of direction is completed and the horse proceeds in the opposite direction.

B 4
Decreasing and Increasing
the Circle — Spiral

FELIX BÜRKNER says: 'The most important, and unfortunately nowadays too often neglected work "in position" and subsequent two-track movements,* is built upon decreasing and increasing the circle size. The lateral curve of the horse's spine around the rider's inside leg necessary for these movements results in releasing the inside rein in the inside position and an increased feeling of the outside rein, which rein gradually becomes the direct rein.' About four to six months after beginning training of the young horse, and after he has learned to carry himself in the shortened working trot and can understand and react to the lateral aids, work on decreasing and increasing circles — the spiral — can begin.

Purpose: See above.

Aids: The rider makes the circle smaller at a shortened working trot by slightly increasing and shifting the weight to the inside. Inside rein and outside leg work together so that the horse moves sideways forward without the hindquarters being hurried as he moves from the outside toward the centre of the circle. His fore- and hindquarters must be brought simultaneously toward the centre of the circle. Thus, the horse achieves a smaller circle in a gradually contracting spiral curve. This circle must never be smaller than six metres in diameter, as the volte represents the maximum lateral curve of the spine that a horse can execute without losing straightness (evenness) and impairing the gait.

To widen the small circle to a larger one, the rider uses his inside leg slightly behind the girth and his outside rein. The outside rein moves slightly away from the horse's shoulder and leads to the outside. Without relinquishing the seat adapted to the horse's concave bend, the rider's weight is carried in the direction of the movement forwards — outwards.

I have avoided using the pertinent terms 'travers-like' (in connection with decreasing the circle) and 'shoulder-in' (in connection with the movement increasing the circle) because the 'travers' and the 'shoulder-in' are distinct and separate lessons reserved for a later stage of development.

---

*'and the absolute straight fluent gliding into the canter' — I should like to add these words to those of Bürkner.

Fault	*Correction*
Resistance to the true lateral curving of the spine, e.g. while turning to the left, by stiffening the lower jaw and rib cage.	Let the horse yield to the left leg out of a volte while in motion. Encourage the horse to champ the bit. Tilt the horse's crest.
Resistance to the true lateral curving of the spine, (e.g., to the left) through falling away and propping against the outside (e.g., the right) hind leg.	Ride to the right. Let the horse yield to the right leg. This will cause the horse to move his right hind leg straight forward under the load towards the centre of gravity. With his right leg the rider should prevent the horse from letting the right hind leg move sideways.

For the rider to test the accuracy of all the previous training is the horse's continuing readiness to; increase the length of the stride in the working trot (see page 8); a straight, even and energetic canter (see page 48); and, with a more advanced horse a medium trot (see page 61) on a straight line with increased impulsion, absolute purity of gait and with a beautiful carriage.

B 5
Lateral Bending Exercises
(Riding in Position)

ACCORDING TO the authoritative rider of the last decade, Felix
Bürkner, the lateral bending work now follows in the developmental
training of the horse. This goes hand in hand with the perfecting of the
decreasing and increasing spiral circle work and is always alternated with
energetic 'normal' work, riding forwards and frequent change of direction. In addition to this, jumping exercises (see page 70) and cross-
country riding must never be neglected.

Lateral bending exercises are divided into two positions:

(a) The 'first position', so named because it precedes and prepares for
the 'second position':

In the first position, also called 'shoulder fore,' the outside hind foot
tracks the corresponding front foot. However, the inside hind leg by
approximately half a hoof width tracks under and towards the centre of
the horse. Seen from the front, the inside hind foot is visible between the
two front legs. The horse is moving on a so-called 'single' track (not
'widened' as in the two-track movements) and with an even, barely
perceptible lateral bending of the spine through the entire length of his
body. The head is turned slightly to the inside; therefore, away from the
direction towards which he is going. The rider glimpses the horse's inside
eye and nostril. For the time being, this is done at the working trot,
perhaps slightly moderated, but still a working trot. Later, then also at
the collected (shortened) trot, and then the medium trot. For corrective
measures, it can also be done at the canter. (See illustration page 46.)

(b) The 'second position', often simply called 'position':

This is not only (as with the shoulder fore) an exercise to achieve
greater suppleness, but also a preparation for certain exercises which
require increased self-carriage as, for instance, transitions to the collected
canter, two-tracking, contracted turns and the collected walk.

In this second position, in equestrian language also referred to as
'position' or 'second position', the inside hind foot tracks the corresponding front foot. However, the outside hind leg tracks a half hoof width
inside the track of the outside front leg. Seen from the front, the *outside*
hind foot becomes visible between the horse's two front legs. The horse
moves as in the first position on a single track and with a barely percep-

tible lateral bend evenly distributed throughout the whole back structure of the animal. However, the horse's head, contrary to the shoulder fore, is facing the direction of the movement. The rider glimpses the inside eye and nostril. As a lesson (training exercises), riding in 'position' may only be executed at the walk or collected trot. *The purpose of riding in first and second positions* is now self-evident. However, knowing that I risk the accusation of becoming over-theoretical, I will summarize the purpose of bending exercises as follows:

1 To achieve complete, relaxed suppleness in the acceptance of aids. This is only achieved when the hind legs move completely straight and close to one another, under the load in the direction of the centre of gravity. In the words of von Heydebreck, 'Everything depends on this straight forward going.'

Correct forward movement is only completely achieved if there is harmony in the stretching and contracting of the extensor and flexor muscles primarily of the back and stomach. This ideal harmony is achieved through bending work.

2 Further development of the capability and preparation for collection. The way is now open for the impulsion to flow freely from the hindquarters to the forehand. The rider is now able by means of this impulsion to improve collection.

3 The possibility of preparing the horse for lessons requiring a lesser or greater degree of collection and through this readiness to assure the quality of their execution. As an example the classical transition from the second position into the even cadence collected canter, gliding into that gait from the inside leg.

4 Preparation for two-tracks.

Aids in Riding the First Position (shoulder fore): Horse's head slightly to the inside. Rider's inside seat bone pushed forward. Slightly shortened inside rein and rider's inside leg active; maintain the yielding of the corresponding side of the horse. As soon as yielding to the inside rein is achieved, the outside rein comes into action; and together with the outside leg controls the horse's hindquarters and shoulder. The horse's neck is in line with the very slight lateral bend of the entire spine. The rider's lower back and both legs maintain rhythm and liveliness of the gait. At the beginning a lower neck position of the horse and a slight sideways bend at the poll are tolerated.

Fault	*Correction*
Rider pulls on the inside rein. Therefore, gait becomes dull and lacking in purity of movement.	Lighten contact of inside rein so that hind legs are not hampered in their even, regular forward thrust.

Fault	Correction
Rider sits to the outside.	Inside knee and heel lower — outside shoulder of rider to the fore.
Rider carries his inside hand too far over the withers.	Shorten inside rein. Each hand stays on its own side of the withers.
The horse bends his loose neck in front of the withers only, instead of at the poll.	Go back to the working trot on a straight line and make the horse stretch his neck and assume proper contact. Re-establish suppleness in the poll through driving him onto voltes in an animated gait, and re-establish champing of the bit.
Horse tilts the poll.	See corrections in turn on the forehand (page 15.)
Because he is tired the horse assumes too loose and low a neck carriage.	Do bending work with the young horse before it has become fatigued.

Aids in Riding the Second Position ('Position'): The same as in the first position, however with greater application of the outside aids so that the horse's head is bent in the direction in which he is going and the outside hind foot is placed one half a hoof's width inside the track of the corresponding fore foot. The horse's voluntary bend at the poll must be the result of the rider's leg aids; the hands must only hint.

Fault	Correction
The horse's head position has been forced by a too strong hold or pull on the inside rein. The gait is without expression and is not true.	Lighten contact, so that hind legs are not hampered in their even, regular forward thrust.
The horse bends his loose neck in front of withers only, instead of at the poll.	See corresponding correction in 'first position.'
Horse resists bending at the poll.	See above.
Horse resists lateral bending of the rib cage.	Cease collection and 'position' and resume work on the circle.
Horse puts his hindquarters to the inside travers-like and goes on two tracks.	Less influence of outside controlling leg. Pulling or fixing of inside rein will also produce this resistance of the horse, in which case use a lighter, more subtle influence of the inside hand (see corresponding correction in 'riding in first position' page 42).

Riding in the first and second positions is also performed in the

OUTSIDE OR COUNTER POSITION

The horse is now flexed to the outside of the school, and therefore must move with the opposite lateral flexion of his spine.

Aim: To sharpen obedience and make the horse more attentive to the outside aids. Preparation for counter shoulder in, renvers and outside (counter) canter. Correction for falling away through the outside shoulder or outside hind foot.

Aids: Similar to those for riding in the first or second position, except in the turns. (Do not forget that the 'inner' (concave) spinal flexion is now towards the outside of the school.) In the corners the outside feet describe a slightly smaller arc than the inside ones. Therefore, their forward motion must be restricted through the leading outside rein so that the inside hind foot is able to follow and the pure rhythm of the gait is maintained.

The turns must not be too tight and should be ridden with only a slight suggestion of the poll bent to the side.

General comments about seat and aids in the lateral bending exercises and the two-track work discussed later: Rider's seat adjusts with suppleness to the lateral flexion of the spine. Hips and shoulders of the rider are parallel to the hips and shoulders of the horse. Thus, as in the turn, the seat bone on the concave inner (and almost imperceptibly lower) side of the horse is pushed well forward with a low knee and heel down.

There must never be even pressure between inside and outside legs when they are in exact alignment. They would work one against the other, each would negate the influence of the other. Therefore, the rule: Inside leg slightly behind the girth; outside a little more behind the girth.

According to the basic rule of 'going along with the movement,' the rider always keeps his centre of gravity over the centre of gravity of the horse (neutral seat).

LATERAL BENDING EXERCISES

'Volte' and 'Working on the curb'
Lateral bend in the volte of six metres diameter in a collected
canter to the right. Rider is using the curb only.

Introducing lateral spinal flexion
Second position, term commonly abbreviated to 'position.' The lateral bend of the spine must be completely uniform to the point of croup.

LATERAL BENDING EXERCISES

Counter position

First position (shoulder fore) left. Outside hind leg and outside foreleg are aligned. Inside hind leg is approximately a half a hoof's width inside the track of the inside foreleg. It is visible between the two forelegs.

B 6
Working canter

IT IS just as difficult to define a specific length of stride for the working canter as it is for the working trot. Strides at the canter, just as those at the trot, will vary with each horse.

Prerequisite: The horse must be able to carry himself in a moderated working trot and must be able to obey the sideways driving aids in the decreasing and increasing spiral circles. Whereas the horse in the open has so far selected his own canter lead, he must now learn in the riding school to take the correct canter lead. The circle size is decreased at a slightly shortened working trot and then increased. Upon re-establishing the original dimension of the circle, preferably on the open side just before reaching the wall, the outside leg supported by the supporting outside rein establishes contact with the convex side of the horse and limits the sideways movement. At the same time, the inside leg drives to the fore. Whip is on the inside shoulder and the familiar voice aid reinforces the request for canter. Inside hand at first gives a little, but nevertheless a slight bending at the poll to the inside must be maintained.

With a relaxed acceptance to the forward driving aids, the horse will now naturally and with certainty find the correct canter lead.

Especially recommended is a second way of breaking into the canter, which is based on the same principle as the first one described. It helps the rider to maintain the straight line of the horse through the control of the inside hind leg. However, this method assumes that the horse through lateral flexion work has achieved a higher degree of suppleness and the ability to become collected.

Method: We take the horse which is going in the shortened working trot on the circle in the shoulder-fore position and give, after a few strides, the above-mentioned aids to canter. At the same time, we reposition the forehand which has moved a little to the inside, and it now returns to its former position on the circle. The slight swing to the outside by the leading shoulder requires a considerable degree of attention and sensitivity on the part of the horse.

Young horses who have been schooled from the very beginning to break into the canter from a widening of the circle or from the shoulder-fore position will, with the application of correct aids, never even dream of breaking into the wrong lead by putting the hindquarters to the inside, a bad mistake, which, once rooted, is almost impossible to erase and which will hinder further progress. In order to prevent this error from sneaking in, we avoid even 'for the sake of learning' the beloved transition to the canter out of the corner.

Aim of Working Canter: To achieve a smooth transition into this gait with minimal use of the aids out of the shortened working trot and later also out of the walk. Certain maintenance of correct lead. Improvement of the carriage of the horse. Preparation for medium and collected canter.

Aids: To commence the canter the described aids should become increasingly hints only. Ultimately only the slightest indication by the inside rein and a stretching of the inside leg should be necessary. The more quietly this schooling proceeds, the quieter and softer the ensuing canters will be. At the very moment the horse picks himself up for the first canter stride, the rider's hand gives slightly and his lower back and legs direct the flow of the movement. During the canter, the rider follows the forward movement well with a deep seat.

For the time being we do not go directly from the canter back to the walk.

Transition from Canter to Trot: Inside leg and rein the same as for 'first position'. The driving aids ensure that even as the check is taking place the very first strides of the trot will swing freely forward.

During the first exercises in schooling for the canter in the riding school, the horse's natural canter stride should be disturbed as little as possible. Only after a few days should the rider think about the driving and withholding aids from which the characteristic canter tempo, specific to each horse, will be developed.

Half-halts in rhythm, together with predominating driving aids from the rider's inside leg, will achieve an even canter stride. 'One stride like the other.' At the end of approximately 12 months of such training, the working canter can be developed into a medium canter − 350 metres per minute − by bringing the hindquarters more up under the horse.

Whereas with the young horse the first collection in the trot is achieved by a shortening of a swinging, flowing medium trot, the shortening and later the collecting of the working canter is achieved through frequent changes to the canter from a collected walk. The aids are as previously described. Initially allow several transitional walking steps.

Error	*Correction*
Restlessness between changes to the canter.	Golden rule: Do not try to change to the canter again until horse has become entirely calmed down, relaxed and on the aids. To

Error	*Correction*
	help in achieving this, go back to the moderate working trot on the circle, concentrating on turning the shoulders to the inside of the circle thereby achieving relaxation and distracting the horse.
Restlessness and bolting during the canter.	If instability should be the cause of this error: Return to the working trot on the circle. If nervous tension: Frequent and continual changing between shortened working trot and gliding into the canter on the circle. This has both physical and emotional relaxing effect. The more tense the horse, the more relaxed the rider should remain!
The horse loses his straightness and moves in a travers-like fashion. The inside hind leg moves away from the correct track and to the inside of the footprint of the inside foreleg. This error lays a dangerous foundation for many further errors and resistances.	By means of shoulder-fore bring the forehand in line with the hindquarters. During the second year of training: At the counter canter, the same correction. The rider must so bring the horse's shoulders against the riding school wall that he has the feeling of cantering into the wall. Having thus achieved straightness on a shallow bend, return to the normal inside canter. The rider's clinging inside leg sees to it that straightness is not again lost through deviation of the inside hind foot.
The horse comes behind the bit or becomes too heavy in the hand and carries his head too low.	Lighten the contact. Increased driving action of lower back and legs. The horse must be ridden forward in lively yet rhythmic strides. The horse will now carry head and neck higher and lose the false flexion of the neck; the neck will be longer. Constant upward tugs on the reins will only provoke the contrary of what you wish to achieve. Pulling upwards and backwards with the reins would only result in a lower carriage and more opposition downwards.
Horse stiffens in the poll. Horse comes above the hands and becomes heavy on the reins and has no carriage. The favourite sawing on the reins to 'loosen the neck' only has the effect that it kills the last remnant of flexibility in the back and brings the horse completely onto his shoulder.	The acceptance and responses of the bit and the rider's hands, as well as engagement of the poll, must be the results of the drive-on aids with elastic rein contact.
The horse contracts himself tensely with constantly convex back and raised hindquarters. The unflexed	Stronger canter on straight line; energetic use of the whip.

Error	*Correction*
stiff hindlegs do not stride fluently under its body. The rider is made to bend grotesquely with each canter stride through the whipping motions of the hindquarters.	
The horse tenses and contracts himself with a rigid, concave back.	See above.
The gait has lost its main characteristic. Engagement-impulsion-springiness. The hindquarters drag. The horse moves forward in a distinct four-beat, a stiff-legged mover.	
The rider is not pulled forward into the saddle because the horse's back is not oscillating. His inside leg is not firm. The feeling in his hand is wooden and his seat is bouncy.	
The horse takes the wrong canter lead or canters disunited.	Return to a lesser gait, e.g. working trot; and after the horse is relaxed, put straight, and quietly onto the aids, try to change to the canter again from 'position.'

Working canter
Canter to the right, diagonal support.

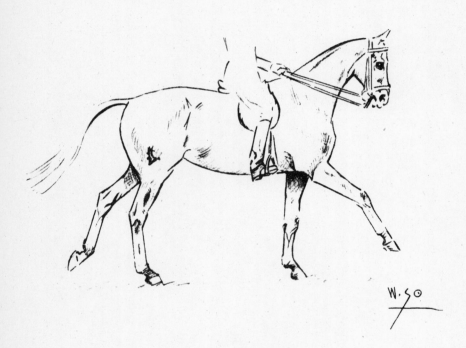

Full-halt and rein-back I

After a half using 'hand-brakes.' The rider attempts to rein-back.
The forehand of this horse which has been jolted into a cringing
posture seems to want to push back the braced hindquarters.

Full-halt and rein-back II

At best, the horse which has been incorrectly prepared for reining-back by a bad halt will give the impression of the forehand pushing the raised hindquarters to the rear. The legs will drag on the ground. The relatively high carriage of the horse is not in keeping with the slight flexion of the hocks.

Full-halt and rein-back III

Standing correctly after a well-executed halt. Hind legs underneath the quarters. From this posture the movement backwards will be completely successful. (See example IV, page 59.)

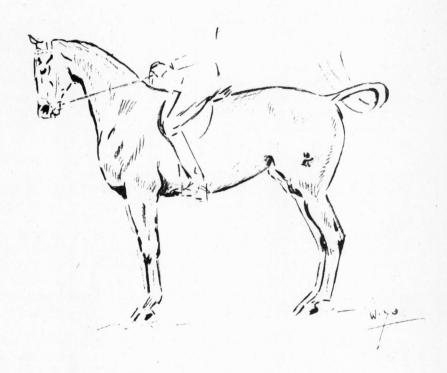

B 7
Rein-Back

THE HORSE moves to the rear willingly, on the bit, with smooth flowing and short strides, without rushing, without hesitation and perfectly straight. The clear and visible sequence of the foot-falls are two-time as in the trot. By repeating the exercise of rein-back and going forward, several times in succession without interruption, loss of rhythm or suppleness, will produce smooth and fluid transitions. For each change of direction the horse should not have his four feet square as in the full-halt. The rein-back seen objectively is a continuation of the halt. Therefore we advise commencing this gymnastic exercise only when the young horse has progressed to more collected exercises including the full-halt (see page 101).

Looking once more at the rein-back entirely from the rider's point of view and reaction: This is a schooling exercise by which the horse's haunches (hip, stifle and hock joints) are flexed. With lowered hindquarters and resilient back, the horse's body is like a taut spring which, by means of the slightest demand of the rider and without change of carriage, fluently and smoothly goes forward again without throwing the upper body of the rider either forward or backward.

The rein-back does not deserve the name if it appears to the observer as though the forehand is dragged back and is pushing the hindquarters to the rear. On the contrary, with the correct engagement and flexion of the hindquarters, the hindquarters take the forehand to the rear. The flexed hind leg 'lifts' the diagonal fore leg. Such a correct posture will create the impression in the observer that the horse while reining-back is in forward movement.

Should a horse be prematurely forced to rein-back, before it has been gymnastically prepared and suppled-up, he will learn various forms of resistance which never would have occurred to him if he had been properly prepared for this exercise.

Purpose: The rein-back and the exercise developed from it, moving alternately forward and backward without hesitation, is a means to and simultaneously a proof of achievement of the harmonious interaction of driving and restraining aids. In other words, responsiveness and suppleness. It enhances collection in that it supples and flexes the joints of the hindquarters and improves the horse's carriage.

Properly ridden, it is no less a criterion of the enthusiastic readiness and responsiveness to the aids than is a willingness to increase speed.

Finally, it also serves as an effective punishment for disobedience in jumping. However, the rider must always be aware when reining-back as a punishment, that any forcing will result in damage to the hind legs and their joints.

Aids: For schooling exercises in reining-back, the rider applies the same aids to the horse on the bit as those that he uses to cause the horse to move forward. (See page 85.) However, the hand intervenes at the precise moment when one hind leg is elevated and the hand resists to the extent that this leg and the corresponding diagonal front leg are then placed to the rear instead of to the front. At that moment, the tightening of the rein must immediately be released. These aids are repeated for as many steps as the rider has previously determined to rein-back (six at the most!) Increased effect of the rider's lower back in proportion to the degree of giving of his hands must achieve either an immediate halt or forward motion without any side stepping. The rider should have no difficulty in keeping his upper body vertical during this movement.

To help the young horse to understand what is being asked during the first lessons in reining-back, it is advantageous to start with a turn on the forehand; and at the moment when a hind foot is lifted increase contact on the rein on that side.

For horses with weak hindquarters and sensitive backs, the rider adopts a lighter seat and places his body, with taut back muscles, slightly in front of vertical.

Error	*Correction*
Horse resists reining-back by bracing his hind legs against the movement.	Collect the horse in forward movement so as to cause him to flex his hind legs underneath him. Now with hindquarters engaged, repeat the aids for reining-back.
The horse rushes backwards, without waiting for the aids and with long strides, away from the seat of the rider. The neck is too low and the poll stiff. The horse is no longer 'on' the aids but 'behind' them.	Put the horse onto the aids by pushing him forward. Then ask for only a few steps backward; but each step must be the result of the aids and not an anticipation or an evasion of them. The rider must feel in his hand the readiness of his horse to move forward at the moment the rider's seat tautens and his fingers open, with the horse happily accepting the bit.
Horse moves to the rear with hind legs spread (one can hardly call it reining-backwards), and thereby avoids full engagement of the hocks which would come from the proper acceptance of the weight.	Through work on the circle, achieve more flexion of the hind legs individually, and so increase their carrying capacity.

Error	*Correction*
Horse becomes crooked by letting one hind foot evade to the outside.	Cure of the symptom: Rein-back along the wall, placing the evading hind leg nearest the wall. Temporarily use a wider opening of the reins on the corresponding side. With the shoulder-outward, bring it in line with the evading hind leg, forcing the latter to take up the weight. Academic, theoretical correction and permanent cure: Work on the circle and lateral bending work.
Sliding to the rear, the forelegs dragging because weight is on the forehand, at the same time, however, with elevated quarters from stiff stifles and joints.	By means of working trot on the circle, the hindquarters will be made to bend and carry the weight. Lateral bending work. The weight bearing hind legs must 'lift' the corresponding forelegs!
Horse steps back without proper carriage with low neck and head position.	Before reining-back, engage the hocks by collecting the horse in forward movement. Without flexed hocks, of which the visible indication among others, is that the poll is carried at the highest possible point, the exercise of reining-back is of no gymnastic value whatsoever.

Full-halt and rein-back IV

In the correct execution of the rein-back the flexed hocks under the
hindquarters carry the lightened forehand to the rear. The legs
move in diagonal sequence in expressive half strides. The high
carriage is the result of the flexed hindquarters.

Medium trot

At the medium and extended trot, the imprints of the hind feet must mark a narrow track; the stifle must be brought forward and upwards energetically to allow the leg room for a good forward thrust.

If the horse moves wide behind with legs spread, which cannot be seen from the side; the forward reach of the strides (walking and trotting) exceeds that to the rear, then the hocks are not being flexed to carry the weight and the horse's effort will be from the shoulder.

B 8
The Medium Trot

IF AFTER about nine months of training, the young horse's croup, back and stomach muscles have become strengthened, and the impulsion of the hindquarters and their capacity for flexing developed by the bending exercises are assured, the medium trot can be practised for short periods.

The medium trot is an intensification of the working trot with respect to ground coverage (approximately 300 metres per minute), carriage and expression; and is in the middle between collected (see page 91) and extended trot (see page 144).

The medium trot is not a working gait, but as a schooling gait and an aid to the gymnastic development it is essential. (See 'Purpose'.)

The characteristic feature of the medium trot is the lengthening and energetic action of the strides. Since this is achieved through the rider's balance and through the flexion of the hocks, the forehand is enabled to lift and extend the forelegs with complete freedom. The forefeet touch the ground at the spot where the toes point to at the moment of highest elevation. The action of the forehand must, with the utmost of precision and expressiveness remain round and fluent. Cramped and choppy stretching of the forelegs indicate false tension. (See 'Error'.)

The horse extends on the bit, with the nose slightly ahead of the vertical in a beautiful carriage; and allows the impulsion to flow from the rear to the front through the poll. This impulsion is regulated by the rider's hand supported by the action of his lower back and is transmitted as needed to the horse's joints to serve as a spring or to the bracing weight of the hindquarters. The elastic impulsion of the hindlegs forward and upward is primarily and initially a result of their flexion and engagement and occurs *before the full extension* of the joints.

Purpose: The improvement of the gait by means of extending thrust and impulsion. Stabilizing the balance, carriage and posture of the horse by means of greater engagement of the hindquarters with resulting flexion of the neck and poll. Confident obedience to the aids.

Last but not least, the medium trot serves as a test of the horse's correct schooling and as a means of eliminating errors resulting from incorrect collection.

Aids: The rider drives the horse by gradually increasing leg aids, assisted when necessary by the whip, from an expressive working trot into a stronger, more balanced movement evenly on both reins. The strides should become longer and more expressive, however the rhythm should remain the same without increasing speed. With the horse's greater acceptance of the bit, the bend of the poll becomes assured. The hindquarters having become lowered in the development of impulsion a higher head and neck carriage results — the relative elevation. The bend at the poll must be maintained; without that, the medium trot will inhibit any advancement and will also damage the joints. At the extended trot the rider should have the sensation of riding uphill, and must not be tossed about by the suppled and oscillating swinging back. The 'glued-to-the-horse' rider is the hallmark of a horse with a 'swinging-back' in contrast to the appearance resulting from an incorrect 'stiff-legged' moving horse.

To begin with, this exercise should be done only for the briefest of periods, occasionally perhaps through the diagonal of the riding school. For horses with a weak back, the rider should commence at first with rising trot. Corners should be round and not tight.

Error	*Correction*
The horse bores on the bit. The hind legs push too hard and the whole weight is pushed onto the forehand.	Frequent transitions between the medium trot and working trot. The necessary half-halts will cause the horse to yield more to the bit, become more responsive to the reins, so that the hindquarters are obliged to carry more of the weight.
The horse hurries when asked to lengthen the stride, becomes irregular and carries his neck and head too high, without using his back.	Calmly return to the working trot! Increase it only after the long, rhythmic strides have been re-established and after the horse accepts the hand and resumes oscillation of the back.
The forelegs stretch in a stiff and jerky motion. The fore feet touch the ground behind the spot at which the toes pointed at the moment of highest elevation. Nevertheless, in spite of or maybe because of this, the gallery will applaud!	Decrease the tension on the rein.
The gait becomes passage-like, floating, with a taut, unyielding back. Admiring reaction from those on the ground!	Through energetic working trot with an oscillating back, re-establish the liveliness of the gait.
The hind legs are spread instead of being close together and tracking in the hoof marks of the forefeet. By this	To cure the sympton: a more opened (leading) rein. Training correction: lateral bending work.

Error	*Correction*
'paddling' they evade carrying the weight and bending.	
The horse falls apart and starts to forge.	A tired horse ought not to be asked to do the medium trot.
The rider is left behind the movement.	The rider's upper body should go along more with the movement.

Medium trot

The so-called medium trot of a 'stiff-legged mover'. The hind legs strike off too far back and push the weight onto the forehand. When the horse moves off, the shoes of the hind feet are visible too much and for too long. The hocks swing to the rear and upward in the direction of the tip of the tail, instead of *forward* and upward. The horse resembles a swimming duck, whose webbed feet pushing to the rear are used for propulsion only, the weight being carried by the water.

The horse's depressed back is not moving elastically but is held down rigidly. Its deepest point − a 'hollow' − is just slightly behind the withers. The rider is unable to sit down to the contracted back and is thoroughly tossed about; the rider 'looks down' and rides holding his hands as if he were playing the piano.

Medium canter

Turn to the left at the medium canter. The lateral bend of the horse's spine and the position of the rider have adjusted themselves to the flatter curve which corresponds to the tempo of medium canter.

B 9
Medium Canter

AS SOON as the horse moves off into the canter surely and evenly from the working trot and in the working canter keeps his balance, he can then, in the open and on a straight line, gradually be asked for a medium canter (about 350 metres per minute); this gait is between the collected (see page 95) and the extended canters (see page 149).

The characteristic of the medium canter is a swinging, ground covering regular series of strides. The horse's outline becomes longer, the contact more definite, the collection and elevation less than in the collected canter. However the lively and even rhythm of the strides remains the same. Carriage and submission must not be lost. In spite of the horse being more on the bit, he must not look for support from the hand.

At the completion of one year's training, the medium canter can be extended, on suitable springy turf, in order to strengthen heart and lungs to a speed of approximately 500 metres per minute, with the rider now in a forward seat. A quiet and low use of the reins, so as not to interfere with the impulsion of the hindquarters or action of the back, thus making it easier for the horse to 'gallop into a lengthening position of the neck.'

Purpose of the medium canter: Transition to the working and extended canters. Increase of impulsion and the accelerating action of the hindquarters, as well as suppleness. The horse is encouraged to use his back more. Preparation for the collected canter, as the medium canter intensifies the spring which will be useful for the shortened gait.

Aids: The transition between the working and the medium canter should be fluent and unhurried. The drive-on aids must not be abrupt. When necessary, through easy cadenced half-halts, maintain submission, the liveliness of the mouth, and the evenness of stride.

The stronger the pace, the more the rider should follow with his seat. Frequently canter on a loose rein or without contact. The rider learns thereby to hold his horse with a completely independent seat, and the horse learns to use every opportunity to stretch. The manner in which the rider rides the corners at the medium canter with a long rein, horse extending his neck but still on the bit, is an indication of the rider's seat and the balance of the horse.

Error	*Correction*
The horse's neck retracts. Because of this, the oscillation is unable to flow freely from behind through the neck towards the horse's mouth.	With a free and lower rein, drive the horse energetically forwards and canter him into a longer neck.
The canter strides begin to drag. Back is no longer oscillating sufficiently.	Cure for the symptom: Practise the canter going uphill to increase push from behind and thus promote the activity of the back.
Canter strides are shuffling and too hasty.	Cure for symptom: Same as above, except work downhill.
When using half-halts in order either to maintain evenness of tempo when the horse is getting away or to shorten stride, the rider controls the horse with reins only. This cause the horse to drag under stiffening hindquarters and the impulsion is restrained.	Do not try to control the canter stride by pulling on the reins. Maintain the fluent impulsion of the bent hindquarters with your back and leg aids.

B 10
Work at the Walk II
THE MEDIUM WALK

FROM THE first day of schooling, the free walk with loose rein has been practised. As the horse learned to stretch, seek and champ the bit, that walk gradually developed into a free walk on a long rein. If the hoof prints remained even, we then attempted with reins taken up to achieve intermittent light contact. This contact came about naturally when slowing down from the trot to the walk when the horse remained on the bit through the action of the faster gait maintained by the rider's legs lightly pressed to the horse's sides. We practised this new combination at the walk for only very brief periods, so as not to lose the free forward movement. If the strides become hasty and shorter, we immediately returned to a free rein.

After about a year's training, when carriage and suppleness have been secured through trotting and canter work, these intermittent exercises in walking on the shorter rein will result in an ever more definite and certain contact. The strides are free, rhythmic and long (about 125 metres per minute). The horse appears keen and relaxed. Hind feet step beyond the tracks of the forefeet. The horse is now moving at medium walk, midway between the collected (see page 151) and the extended walk (see page 153).

Purpose: Foundation for the later development of the collected and extended walk. For daily use cross-country and in the riding school. The medium walk, just as the medium trot, is proof of the correct foundation and sequence of training and can never be developed from work at the walk exclusively.

Aids: The medium walk, which is a free walk on the bit, should be asked for only when the horse has been warmed up to supple his back, moves onto the bit and allows himself to be driven forward — thus, is not rushing; which at the beginning of the schooling period will be accomplished through work at the trot and the canter, and possibly on an incline or with cavalletti.

To achieve a free and ground-covering forward stride with a lazy horse, stimulating use of the leg is essential. The rider's leg action is in rhythm with the gait with barely perceptible short alternating taps which may be reinforced by use of the whip immediately behind the leg.

68

The very much loved simultaneous drumming of the legs disturbs the rhythm and with sensitive horses will result in cramping and shortening of the strides.

Continual use of the leg only results in making the horse dull — 'dead' — to the leg aids. If, from time to time, the brief leg aids are not sufficient, it is then necessary, once or twice, to use the leg energetically in conjunction with whip to make the horse more sensitive the leg aids, so that when the rider's seat is well down in the saddle the implication of the ensuing leg action is sufficient to maintain a long fluent stride.

It would be premature at this point in the training of the horse to attempt more collected work at the walk. For this, *the most difficult exercise in riding*, even a talented horse under a superior rider will have to wait until approximately the end of the second year's training.

Error	*Correction*
The walk is restrained and 'wishy-washy', with uneven and too hasty steps. The hind hoof prints do not track those of the forefeet.	Commence by using limbering-up exercises that will relax and stretch the horse. Most important: work on the circle in the working or medium trot, work on the circle in the working canter, working trot, working canter, alternating all the time.
The strides are regular, however not covering enough ground and not energetic enough.	Stimulating, alternating use of the leg.
Rider tries to use his legs, on both sides, with a drumming action to create a wider, more ground-covering stride and make the gait more fluent.	Same as above.

B 11
Training to jump

SO MANY excellent books have been written about the training of the jumping horse, that I would consider it presumptous to go into this speciality of riding more fully. I will therefore only give some hints for schooling to jump insofar as they relate to the training of the ordinary riding horse.

Just as the medium trot and the medium walk are indicative tests of the schooled horse, so is the willing, straight and even, and relaxed jumping over obstacles with an arched neck and spine, the so-called bascule. Therefore, daily jumping exercises go hand in hand with the gymnastic exercises in the arena and riding out in the country. The jumping lessons of the young horse under the saddle must be sharply differentiated from the 'free jumping' used to achieve relaxation and looseness (see page 11) and may never be done before the end of the riding hour when the loose, relaxed horse accepts being driven on — i.e., when the rider can ride the working trot and from working trot into canter on long reins without the horse rushing.

Preparation: At first at a walk, then at a rising trot, over the cavalletti. Should the horse still rush, turn away from the cavalletti in a relaxed manner until he can be driven forward. It is advantageous to turn away more often to the right than the left, as most horses show preference for running out to the left. This is because the horse is more apt to drift out towards the left leg (see 'crookedness' page 16).

Now we are ready to commence with the actual jumping (heretofore, cavalletti were only ridden over not jumped). Set up a cavalletti and then five and a half strides beyond it an oxer one metre wide, the first pole being 50 centimetres high and the second pole 60 centimetres high. (Nominally a combination with an easy spread.) Jump this obstacle at a rising trot. At a trot, because the horse should not make an in-and-out of this exercise, but should learn to stretch himself over the oxer at a trot, following short checks between the two obstacles. And at the rising trot, so that the rider does not bounce on the horse's back and is better able to follow irregular movements. It would not be helpful to set up a rail in place of the oxer. The horse would soon learn to run out.

At the end of the schooling period and after a rest, another and inviting obstacle at the canter. Then repeat the same as at the beginning of the jumping lesson, at a walk over a few cavalletti, and back to the stable.

Aids: The best way we can aid the horse in his jumping will always be to create for him the opportunities and possibilities of finding the means which will assure him clearing the obstacle safely with the least effort.

The first of these possible means is the so-called forward seat, which should be practised frequently. A condition for the correct forward seat is that the rider can ride his horse on the aids in an upright, deep and balanced or normal seat. Then he will also be able to do the same thing in the forward seat, and the horse must be put to and kept on the aids exactly in the same way as he would be for work on the flat.

The scope of this book precludes going into the forward seat any further. Suffice it to say that the fluency of the hips and the closeness of the knees are the most important part. The stirrup, which in the normal seat is merely a support to the foot, becomes more of a prop to the firm leg, which does not move from its position. Just as in the normal schooling seat correct half-halts should draw the seat bones of the rider farther into the saddle and support the back, so in the forward seat the knees should be drawn still more strongly onto and grip the saddle. The lower back brought forward now finds its base and support in this knee grip. In other words, one can and must, in the forward seat, ride exactly the same way as in the balanced seat, with tautened lower back muscles pushing to the front, the difference is only that in the forward seat the driving force of the rider's back is transferred to the sides of the horse through the knee grip instead of through the pressure of the seat bones directly on the horse's back. Moreover, the closer the rider's seat can remain to the saddle, despite the shortening of two or three holes of the stirrup leathers the better and quicker the rider is prepared to use the influence of his seat if the horse should be in any way disobedient. If the horse starts to pull during the approach to the obstacle, the rider allows the horse as much freedom of the reins as he wants without losing contact and without giving up the drive-on aids. At the take-off and during the actual jump over the obstacle, the rider's seat with upper body forward, not exaggeratedly, is lifted out of the saddle. The rider's hands stretch out from the shoulders and elbow joints to the right and left of the mane along the horse's neck in the direction of the horse's mouth, but remain in contact with the mouth. Knee and lower leg stay precisely in their place. Heel is down and the ball of the foot on the stirrup irons.

In the landing, the rider absorbs the jolt in his knee joints, and they take up the weight of his upper body in an elastic fashion so that it does not burden the forehand.

71

A schooling aid to teach the horse to find his take-off point — i.e., to teach him to judge, and also to regulate his tempo — is to set up a cavalletti approximately seven metres before the actual obstacle (a two-element obstacle separated by an easy distance). As we are aware of the size of the strides of the canter in working tempo — single stride about seven metres, double stride about eleven metres — we can achieve a certain and correct take-off. The first canter stride (if seven metres) takes us over the cavalletti. The second one is between the cavalletti and the fence. The third is the take-off. The observer can count one-two-three, and at three the horse will take off.

Before a ditch, it is important not to accelerate the speed too soon (however, the average rider does this only once!). In any event, the last three strides must be ridden with definite emphasis.

Over water and over new obstacles, it is advisable to have a more knowledgeable horse to lead the way.

Should a martingale be considered necessary during the jumping, it is only helpful (when turning) as long as the rein line is not broken. Otherwise, the use of the martingale will have the opposite effect.

With the young horse, after each jump let him continue moving straight forward and slow him up very quietly. Drop the reins, praise.

Jump training

Oblivious to the teachings of Kegel and Séchenyi, this was the type of jumping that you could see approximately at the turn of the century. Even at that time good riders allowed their horse enough head freedom and took a central posture so that the horse was able to achieve a bascule. It was not until Tod Sloan and Caprilli, who died in 1907, that the present racing, cross-country, jumping and all round forward seat was adopted.

Jump training
Perfect bascule. (Drawing from photograph.)

Training to jump

Beautiful concentration which can be seen in the ears and the eyes
of the horse, already looking towards the next obstacle.

Training to jump
The horse confidently lets himself fly.

Training to jump

Even the martingale can, under certain circumstances, in the turns, be useful. However, it certainly must be adjusted with care.

Training to jump
Close clinging leg and knee position of the rider. Low heel. Seat is
not exaggeratedly far out of the saddle. However, the hand should
give a little more in the direction of the horse's mouth. This is the
cause of the minimal bascule

Training to jump

(Cross-country and up-and-down hill work.)

Downhill work. Upper body of rider is at right angles to the horse's back. The reins allow the horse to balance himself by raising and lowering his neck. Close legs avoid any deviation from the desired direction. For climbing uphill, complete freedom of the reins.

To put to the aids

Horse does not move because of the cramped and stiffened poll. It is as though the necessary 'drop of oil' is missing in the joint. Incorrect functioning of the muscles due to stiffened poll causes bulging lower neck. Gait: Pounding in front with nothing following behind.

Faults and Disobediences	*Corrections*
Horse jumps with a stiff back, without the bascule, over the obstacle. Back and neck outline of horse does not form an even curve.	Set up two close cavalletti immediately behind a higher obstacle. As the horse will only see them when he is in the air, he will stretch his neck, and because of the self-preservation instinct push his neck and head forward and downwards; will therefore be in a diving position so as not to land on the cavalletti.
Horse leaves the ground too soon.	Obstacle as above.
Horse leaves the ground too late and does not stretch over the obstacle.	Moderately wide jumps with narrowly laid out cavalletti in front of the obstacle. These cavalletti should be the same colour as the obstacle.
The horse miscalculates his take-off point as it is not sufficiently experienced to negotiate the last strides before the take-off.	See 'judgement' under 'Aids.'
The horse stops in front of the obstacle.	Rein-back the horse to the position where you can ride him towards the obstacle again. This position can also be obtained by turns on the forehand and haunches, but it must be immediately done so that the horse does not have time to think the matter over.
Stopping and rearing.	Turn the horse away to the side in which it is more supple. Drive forward with spur and whip, ideally before the front legs have returned to the ground.
The horse runs out by a quick, half turn.	After a turn to the opposite side, come at the obstacle again and ride at it energetically. It is important to think over whether these and similar disobediences have not occurred because *the obstacles have been made too difficult too soon*. Should this be the case, then an identical but lower obstacle should first be negotiated.
The horse runs out at the obstacle or jumps crookedly.	The running-out horse should be brought to a halt as quickly as possible. Then turn on the forehand in the direction of the approach and take the horse back at a walk to a position from which he can be ridden towards the fence.
	Now place the horse in shoulder-in position — half right if the horse has been running out to the left, half left should the horse have run out to the right. Care must be taken to keep the corresponding rein effect light. Even the slightest 'leaning' on the rein would help the

Faults and Disobediences	*Corrections*
	horse to run out in that direction again. Whilst the rider uses driving aids the opposite hand becomes the supporting rein aid. The same procedure will be followed where a horse jumps crookedly. With such a horse, it is advisable to bring him into the fence at an angle slightly opposite to that in which he is apt to jump.
After the disobedience of a refusal, the horse starts to rein-back.	The rider must correct this disobedience by continuing to rein-back and making it faster, so 'driving out the devil with Beelzebub.' So as not to take the horse too far away from the obstacle, this forced reining-back should be done on a circle. So as to avoid an evasion of the hind legs, it is advisable to carry the reins further apart.
The horse rushes blindly at the obstacle.	Such a temperamental horse or those that have had unpleasant experiences in jumping before, must not be punished with force, but must have an emotional readjustment to bring them more relaxed to the obstacle. As soon as such nervousness is detected near a jump, the horse should be turned away and trotted on a circle, with frequent stroking of the neck and soothing voice.
	This is done at the working trot, occasionally quietly gliding into a canter, until the horse breathes deeply and quietly and stretches himself into the aids and allows himself to be driven forward happily, which is to say that the horse at the signal of the rider, will lengthen his strides without losing rhythm ('stretch into the reins'). Then, when the horse is quiet and least suspects anything, it is taken casually, preferably at a trot, over an inviting and easy obstacle and from there directly to a person with the feed bucket. By this method horses can also be taught not to rush after jumping an obstacle. Eventually, frequent turning away and circling before the obstacle will suffice.
The opposite of the above is the lazy and ungenerous horse.	With such horses it is most effective to use the whip and the spur. At ditches, one allows them to go alongside an energetic lead horse and in general utilizes every opportunity to awaken their sleeping enthusiasm by galloping with others in the open country.

Faults and Disobediences

Faults in the position of the rider: No following of the shoulder and elbows, insufficient grip with the knee, upper body is either in front of or behind the movement of the horse, exaggerated forward position out of the saddle, swinging legs, hands too high, etc.

Corrections

All these errors must be corrected before one entrusts the jumping instruction of a young horse to such a rider.

C

Increasing Collection

Reciprocal action of driving and restraining,
as well as the direct
and indirect aids. Increasing impulsion

C 1

To Put On the Aids

THE FIRST reciprocal action of the aids consists of the rider driving his horse on, by means of his back and leg muscles, from the rear to the front, first into a hand that 'gives' and later a restraining hand.

Now we have reached the state of training in which we can expect not only that the young horse will bring his hindquarters further under himself in order to push off with more energetic and longer strides, but we can also expect him to flex his higher joints, his hocks, and therefore engage the haunches. The restraining hand loosens the poll and the resulting suppleness causes the horse to accept the bit with a closed mouth.

We call this acceptance of both the driving and restraining aids, 'being on the bit.'

The prerequisite for this reaction to the driving aids and the controlling hands simultaneously, is the willingness and the ability of the horse to allow the action of the rider's back and legs to move unimpeded through the joints of his hindquarters and through his back, neck and poll, to the bit; and conversely allow the restraining action of his mouth to flow through the poll, neck and back all the way into the joints of the hindquarters. This willingness and ability we call 'suppleness.'

Errors Which Impede Suppleness	*Correction*
The horse is not supple. He does not transmit the aids to impulsion through the hindquarters, through the poll and mouth, into the rider's hand. Conversely, by stiffening the neck and stiffening the back it does not allow the rein action to affect the joints and the hindquarters.	Changes of speed in the working trot and canter. Half-halts. Lateral bending work.

If the horse accepts the driving aids to impulsion and goes willingly onto the bit, an elastic communication is established between the rider's hands and the horse's mouth. This is called 'contact.' This contact must never be achieved by a pulling back on the reins, but must be achieved by the horse being evenly driven forward onto the bit. The rider's lower back has the job of counteracting any kind of resistance of the horse on its neck

To put on the aids

Above the bit.
Neck held upward and back.

Behind the bit.
False flexion behind the vertical plane.

To put on the aids

False flexion in the neck
in the horizontal plane.

Horse tilts head,
left ear lower.

and mouth, by the appropriate bracing and by the action of the back musculature and legs. Contact will be complete only when the rein aids find a sure support in the rider's posture.

Fault	*Correction*
The horse hangs on the bit. He leans on the hand, is looking for support on the rein, is using the rein as a so-called 'fifth leg' and appears to wish to be held up by the rider's hand. The hindquarters drag and the movement is impeded.	With lower hands, at first with following rein, then slightly restraining, energetically drive the horse forward by means of back and leg aids. The steps of the horse should be lively but not rushed. The carriage of the horse's head and neck will now become higher and with lighter contact the horse's nose will be just slightly in front of the vertical. This so-called 'picking up' will lighten the forehand. The horse regains his self-carriage and with it his free and expressive movement.
The horse is behind the bit. He is behind the rider's hand, does not accept the bit; the horse's chin comes behind the vertical; his forehand is so 'cramped' it looks as though he were trying to bite himself. The rider does not feel any contact beyond the weight of the reins. The shorter, 'compacted' neck, becoming disengaged from the withers and falsely flexed, and the poll is no longer the highest point.	Always keep the nose in front of the vertical, as above. Frequent riding with reins in one hand. Follow with the rein hand without breaking contact. The attempt to make the compacted neck lengthen and bring the nose in front of the vertical by *lifting* rein actions would be a mistake.* The only way of correcting the horse and of improving his carriage is by the rider's use of his loins and leg aids, and never by raising the reins. Anything achieved by raising the hands would result in all communication between the horse's fore- and hindquarters being interrupted by the back just dropping (becoming hollow) behind the withers; which the hindquarters could not follow.
Horse is 'above the bit'. It attempts to evade the hands by star-gazing, head-shaking, and pulling. His head is almost horizontal and the underneath of the neck is curved forward.	The communication from the hindquarters to mouth and from mouth to hindquarters is interrupted when the concave upper part of the neck obstructs the transmission of the driving and restraining aids and allows them to dissipate as though through a valve. Correction must be achieved by patient lengthening of the horse forward and downward. By this means, the bulging of the lower neck muscles will eventually disappear, as they no longer stretch and strain themselves to push the head upwards.

---

*Monteton said: 'The natural man does everything wrong.' According to the law of action and reaction, a hand pulling upward would only result in increased counter-pressure downward, the error becoming still greater.

C 2
Raising of the Forehand

THE RAISING of the forehand is a characteristic and a result of collection. It is the by-product, not in itself the aim, of the dressage training. It comprises a developing elevation of poll, neck and withers out of the shoulders as a result of a lowering of the flexed hindquarters and the passively resisting rein.

This (relative) raising becomes a direct or active raising at the moment in which the hand through light aids on the reins improves the overall posture of the horse. The indicating rein aids are necessary because most horses lack an innate motivation to offer more than a relative raising of the forehand; maybe there are some who are especially outgoing and take it as their happy duty to collect themselves.

The degree of raising of the forehand cannot be described by any schematic formula. It is dependent on the rideability, the conformation, and temperament of each individual horse, and is a function of the greater or lesser engagement of the haunches. The raising of the forehand will have been achieved in its appropriate degree if the horse in complete suppleness moves with animation through the poll and onto the bit.

Aids: They must be so accurate and balanced that the neck, working as a lever does not lower the back directly behind the withers, but fully engage it in the region of the loins.

Error	*Correction*
Gait and rhythm become impure and lack expression.	An effort to regulate the gait and rhythm by means of rein aids alone would be a superficial cure with devastating effects.
	Above all the rider must have created prerequisites which make it possible to put the horse correctly on to the aids (page 85.)
Rider is unable to sit in the saddle. He feels a faulty sinking of the back immediately behind the withers at the pommel of the saddle, and a hollowing and flattening of the horse's body between his legs; he no longer has a horse between his legs. These are both	The raising of the neck has been forced and too high. Reduce the demands.

Error

Correction

true signs indicating that the horse's hind legs are no longer really under the now rigidly held concave back, and that the limits of the raising of the neck, for which the rider is responsible, have been exceeded. The ability of the hindquarters to carry and flex is no longer equal to carrying the burden, and the hind legs escape the pressure by evading to the rear.

C 3
The Collected Trot

THE HORSE moves completely supple, more elegantly and covering less ground than in the working trot. The flexing of the hocks is greater, and consequently he carries himself higher in front with lighter contact.

The *development* of the collected trot is best achieved after a good medium trot has been executed, by gradually shortening the strides. At the same time it is important to retain lively yet cadenced steps flowing from a supple shoulder, and the impulsion achieved at the medium trot. The impulsion now is more elevated rather than forward. The engaged hindquarters to which the weight has shifted 'lifts' the forehand and makes possible its elegant, round movement. The collected trot, as the extended trot (see page 144), can only be asked for in the second year of training.

Purpose: The most valuable gait to perfect the suppleness, posture and the ensuing capability for collection. Use in all two-track movements.

Just a few words more to characterize correct collection and how the rider will feel it when it has been achieved. Thanks to the lithe play of the swinging back muscles in rhythm with the movement, the rider will feel himself effortlessly drawn down into the saddle so that his seat and legs remain in position. The horse completely accepts the elasticity of the rider's back and legs, that it is an easy task to lengthen and lower the strides, and extend the scope of the horse's neck at will. (See lengthening stride on the bit, page 85.)

Through the energy of impulsion mobilised from within himself, the horse is now prepared, in his physique and emotional attentiveness, to respond instantly to the slightest indications to change his tempo, posture, direction or gait.

Aids to the Collected Trot: With braced back and knees down, legs immediately behind the girth, the rider asks the horse to move his hind legs energetically. The sensitive hand keeps the mouth fresh. The poll appears to have been oiled to complete flexibility. The horse is straight! The collected trot should only be done for short periods and always followed by more free gait variations in between.

Fault	*Correction*
Steps become flat, without flexion of hocks and stifle, and lose their expression.	Re-establish swinging action of the back and contact by forward movement; i.e., put the horse on the aids (see page 85) and restore the proper movement. Then the lost energy and cadence will re-establish themselves.
The horse leans on the hands. Is 'over the bit.'	First employ the corrections explained on page 87. Then, if still necessary, add the half-halts with energetic leg aids.
Horse goes 'behind the bit.'	First employ the corrections explained on page 88. Energetically increase the tempo. Re-establish the contact. When again asking for collection, be very cautious when shortening.
Hindquarters drag.	Energetic increase with driving legs.
Floating, *passage*-like strides.	With less collection, drive forward. Energetic strides. Very gradually, with a light hand, try to shorten again. As soon as the rhythm slows, immediately drive forward and re-establish the oscillation of the back.
By the transition from the halt or the walk to the collected trot, the first strides are not true and are not positive trotting strides.	Before you start the movement, put the horse correctly on the aids as explained on page 85.

The collected trot

Rider is attempting to attain a collected trot on a horse which is not yet ready for collection. Result is an incorrect shortened, but not collected, trot.

Hindquarters stiffen and become too high due to the unflexed hocks. The back does not swing and its deepest point is directly behind the withers. Thus the saddle has slipped forward. The horse (see the look on his face) is resisting the predominant rein aids of the rider whose inactive legs just hang down. The gait is dull and expressionless.

93

The collected canter
Canter to the right

C 4
The Collected Canter

IF AT the beginning of the second year's training the horse has learned to carry himself in the medium canter, we can start to develop the collected canter. The horse must show the ability, by fluid strides out of the engaged and flexed and increasingly weight-bearing hindquarters, to be ready at any moment to respond to the command to canter forward smoothly out of collection into long, free strides.

The succession of the strides should be seen always as a true three-beat gait. They cover less ground, but are instead more elegant than in the working canter.

It is not simply the shortening of the stride that is characteristic of the collected canter, but the elastic spring of the hindquarters coming farther under which gives the rider the pleasant feeling that he is sitting in a well-sprung vehicle on a smooth highway. This feeling results from the flexion of the hocks absorbing the shock of the thrust which makes possible a comfortable, effortless posture in the saddle. The horse is now ready to go on.

Equally important is the absolute straightness, inside hind leg following precisely in the tracks of the inside fore leg, outside hind leg following somewhat inside the tracks of the outside foreleg. This reflects the natural light lateral and longitudinal bend of the spine.

Purpose: Promotes the good carriage of the horse and the flexion in the hindquarters. It makes possible correct control from the canter to walk or halt, as well as tight turns.

Aids: The rider, having prepared the horse to be relaxed and having reached the point where he can be driven — in other words, when the second position has been achieved — will now go into the canter on the circle, at first from the collected trot, later from the shortened walk* with firm contact. It would be wrong, for the time being, to try to achieve a collected canter by shortening the more free cadence of the medium or working canter, as conversely, we have achieved, with the greatest

---

*The shortened, collected walk, being the most difficult lesson, can be achieved only at the very end of the horse's training.

success, the collected trot by shortening the active tempo of the medium trot.

The aids for the canter depart of the completely straight horse should be limited to a short, downward pressure of the rider's close inside leg, an outside controlling leg aid is necessary, and light inside rein to indicate the direction. These aids for the canter depart should be lessened more and more and become mere indications. The rider's seat with taut back remains neutral. This means that the rider keeps his centre of gravity in line with that of the horse. This will result in the weight of his inner seat bone stretching down on the horse's concave side slightly more.

It is particularly helpful, later on, to break into the collected canter without any transitional steps after a turn on the haunches on the circle. Then having achieved the rounded canter strides forward and to the front, maintain them straight and sure!

Once the horse can execute the transition into the collected canter easily and with minimal aids and holds it on his own, he can progress to the collected canter out of the medium canter. Here it is essential to take advantage of the leverage effect of the horse's elevated neck.

For Aids to be used when going to the collected canter from the halt, see page 101. Before starting have the horse's hind legs well engaged, underneath his quarters. At first you can allow a few walking steps in the transition.

The transition from the canter to the trot: Inside leg aids keeping the horse straight, supported by the inside rein, lead to a shoulder-fore type of position. Outside rein aids assist by small half-halts, and with the pressure to the inside keep the shoulder in front of the inside hindfoot. All this fluently without any jerking. For a gentle transition to the walk as means to simple change of leg (see page 138): as above, only that the halt (see page 101) must be completed to such a point that the horse goes immediately into the walk. During the two or three walking strides, change the position and fluently break into the new canter lead.

Fault	Correction
The rider is trying to shorten the strides from medium canter to collected canter with the reins only. From this predominance of the restraining aids, the horse drags its hindquarters and loses impulsion.	Stronger leg and back aids and a hand that gives allow the hindquarters to come more under the horse.
The sequence of the stride is lost. The horse is 'running-along' instead of 'springing' and pushing off in time. He drags his hindquarters along.	Always include brief periods at a free canter to encourage the horse to swing his back. Once this has been re-established, further correction as above.

Fault	*Correction*
Strides are irregular (not in sequence) and uneven.	Half-halts with the outside rein in rhythm with the stride without coming to a standstill midway. Also, predominating driving aid with the inside leg will improve the regularity of the canter stride.
Horse nods in rhythm with the canter.	With a supple flexion of the hocks, the horse has no longer any reason to try to keep his balance by tossing his head up and down (see thrusting the back upward).
Horse's quarters swing to the inside. The inside hind leg no longer tracks on the same track as the inside foreleg. In other words, the inside hind leg comes to inside of the track.	Shoulder-fore type of straightening by putting the shoulders in front of the hindquarters. First position (see page 41). If this crookedness is allowed to continue it will be the root of innumerable faults in the future.
The horse rushes.	More positive, and relaxed strides by frequently going into the canter from the walk.
Canter strides become bounding, lively cadence is lost. The horse stiffens in the poll, in the hips and in the stifle joint; and he unduly uses instead the hocks and fetlock joint.	Going into a canter frequently from the walk will secure and maintain the correct flexion of the hocks. Beforehand, establish engagement by going on a larger circle with energetic transitions from working to strong canter, and vice versa.
The rider is forced to bend unduly with each stride, because the horse's stiffened hind legs result in a vertical rocking motion of the back.	Same as above.
The rider uses inner rein too much. So that the neck is unduly bent in front of the withers, and the horse falls away onto the outside shoulder.	Keep outside rein predominant. Inside hand lighter. Allow the movement to be more free.
Uneven physical development of the horse's two sides. This is shown, for instance, in the canter left strides being slower than the canter right strides.	This deficiency in lateral suppleness can be corrected only with movements in a free gait which allow the horse first to stretch; and then in two-track movements (see page 41, as well as movements described on pages 120, 126).
Of his own accord the horse shortens his stride in the riding of figures, for instance, the volte. The strides become disorganized and jerky because the impulsion is variable and not maintained.	In these more advanced and demanding movements the rider must avoid trying to re-establish impulsion from the bent hocks. He must first ride on a larger circle where he can exercise more energetic transitions from the working canter to the medium canter until the horse gets back 'into full swing' in the real sense of the words.

C 5

The Counter Canter

HAVING ACQUIRED the correct self-carriage in the collected canter, particularly in the corners of the arena, we can now progress to the counter canter. The horse is curved and canters in this position with the outside fore leg leading on a simple track. He therefore is going against his natural bend and position.

After building up the horse's intial confidence and early preparation (see below), we can progress most easily to the counter canter by moving out of the second corner of the long side in a fairly tight change of direction without changing lead. Until the horse is assured in this movement, all corners will be ridden as on a large circle. The rider devotes his special attention to the preservation of a pure and fluent sequence of the canter movements and also to the correct distribution of his own weight so that by being with the movement the rider disturbs the movement of the horse's back as little as possible.

The best way to introduce this movement to give confidence and to practise the counter canter is to ride very flat serpentines (page 24), without changing the position, in a large arena. Errors which occur, including cross-lead or flying changes, are overlooked by the rider who will follow the horse's movement flexibly and respond simply and smilingly by moving the horse onto the appropriate large circle where the horse will 'rediscover for himself' the original movement.

Any form of punishment for the unasked-for change of lead, even one rough check before a new canter depart, will, in the future prove to be disastrous when the rider wishes to introduce flying changes.

Should no large arena for riding be available, the exercise will have to be done in the riding school; perform a half volte and reverse, in the first corner on the short side at the walk or collected trot. At the completion of half volte and returning to the track on the diagonal, canter. Later on do a change in direction on the diagonal of a half school with no change of lead. Eventually this change into the counter canter should be able to be performed on a straight line. The counter canter should also be maintained on the circle or even on the figure 8. In the last two movements as well as in all other turns, the slight curvature of the horse remains that of the counter canter, to the outside and not that of the circle.

Purpose: Best way to prevent any crookedness that may creep in unnoticed in work at the canter or to correct and eliminate it. This is done by skilful placement of the horse's shoulders in the direction of the wall (as though one wished to ride right into it) and in front of the inner hind leg which thus becomes unable to evade; or — what is more or less the same — repeatedly to go along the long side of the wall in counter canter, so that, e.g., one canters to the right on the left lead with the horse's shoulders straight, and vice versa. This results in better control of the inside hind leg, and also results in more being required of the outside hind leg so that the lively action and spring of the whole hindquarters is enhanced.

Preparation for two-track work, particularly the *renvers* and the *travers* at the canter.

Heightening of obedience, collection, self-carriage, and activity of the horse. Improvement of influence, sensitivity and hands of the rider.

Improving the horse's hardiness for stadium jumping with tight turns which have to be ridden at high speed. It is clear that the counter canter in practical use in cross-country or jumping is never asked for in collection as it is in training in the riding school. On the contrary, at such times the horse should be asked to canter in free easy strides, on long reins; a rule which has great merit for the flying change (see page 138).

Aids: These correspond in every way to normal aids for each particular canter lead. The lateral bend of the horse's spine is around the inside leg, in this case the leg closer to the wall. As for the inside canter, the positioning of the horse for the counter canter requires that he is put into the required position before asking for the canter depart.

The rider must be particularly attentive to the curvature of the horse during the turns in the corners, which at first must not be taken too close or too tight, and that the even, fluid three beat of the stride is maintained. Therefore see that the impulsion has been developed before the turn, since even perfectly aligned hindquarters must describe a somewhat larger circle and canter against the normal flexion, which modifies the horse's impulsion. By means of a lightly controlling hand on the outside rein which lightens the horse's forehand supported by driving aids which alternate tactfully with the rein effects, the rider thus maintains the impulsion and the roundness of the canter which would otherwise be lost in the positioning of the turn and result in the horse stumbling into a dull and dragging four beat.

In the course of further schooling at the counter canter, the hocks will become ever more flexible and strong, the counter canter turns ever more fluent and balanced. The previously necessary and often supervisory controlling aid of the outside leg to prevent the change of lead can be eliminated, and the harmonious distribution of weight will become habit.

The rider also now feels each single hind hoofbeat in his fingers. The horse is balanced between the outside leg and the inside rein, which complement one another in diagonal aids. The inside leg and outside rein, however, support this balance as regulators of straightness and carriage as needed, by the inner rein or outer leg, and take care that the halts do not fall on the outside shoulder.

The final test of the horse's schooling and rider's aids in collected canter is a figure 8 with no change of lead on the short side of the riding school.

Fault	*Correction*
The horse is cantering crookedly with the hindquarters to the inside of the riding school.	Place the forehand, in the shoulder-fore position, in front of the inside hindfoot (which is turned toward the wall) as if one intended to canter into the wall, so that the horse remains set straight and on a single track (see 'Purpose').
In the corners the horse loses impulsion and goes into a four beat.	Increase and keep impulsion of the horse *before* you reach the corner.
The horse seeks to free himself from the compulsory position by a flying change without and before being asked for it.	This fault occurs if you ask the horse to change from counter canter to the normal canter before the counter canter is fully established. It is best to correct this over-eagerness by asking for the change from the outside canter to the normal canter only on the diagonal through the whole school, or half-school.
The above fault is committed in the corner.	Flatten the corners. At first, allow a renvers movement. If necessary, ask for this with outside rein and leg. Remain still in the saddle.

C 6
Full-Halts and Standing Square

TRUE TO the law of cause and effect, the execution of a *schooled* full-halt can be achieved correctly only after the horse performs the collected trot and collected canter properly balanced and with self-carriage! This is why we start to speak about the full-halt only at this point.

First of all, to make absolutely clear the vast difference between the half-halt discussed on page 33, and the full-halt:

Half-Halt: Depending on whether, on the one hand, we are talking about the transition to a lower gait or a variation of tempo within the same gait; or, on the other hand, we are talking about the improvement of carriage *without* modifying the tempo, the rein aids will be mainly either a light 'give and take' or by maintaining a steady contact. In both cases, however, the drive-on leg effects will outlast and overrule those of the rein. The horse will not come to a complete halt.

Full-Halt: Here the horse is brought by means of a well-balanced drive-on and resisting aids to a complete standstill from whatever gait he is moving in, moved from behind to the front, absolutely straight. In this case, the rein (restraining) influence outlasts and overrules the drive-on aids, in contrast to the half-halt.

Purpose of the Full-Halt: Cessation of any gait concluding with the full-halt. Increasing suppleness. Preparation and making the horse receptive to the rein-back, a movement contrary to its nature, and which is a continuation of halting.

Aids: A series of half-halts (see page 33), with alternating completely resisting and taking-and-giving rein aids until a full-halt is achieved.

With regard to the interplay of all aids, a full-halt will result from the walk in the following manner: driving the hindquarters forward under the horse and then by bilateral leg pressure holding the quarters. Full seat aids by tightening the lower back with a vertical upper body and resisting hand. If necessary, augmentation of resisting rein aids by more or less taking up on the reins. All this without changing the position of the upper body and passive leg aids. Having achieved the halt in an easy movement from the bent hind legs which are slightly under the horse there is a slight relaxing of the rider's back, and a practically unnoticeable leaning back of the upper body, which results in the back gently pushing the horse onto the bit; and on the other hand also weighs down the hindquarters and keeps them firmly in the position required. At the same time there is an almost invisible giving of the hand so that the horse halts on the bit and stands more freely and with less tension. This ends the horse's impulsion and makes it easier for him to maintain this position.

At the halt the horse should be standing erect, completely straight, and have its weight distributed equally on all four legs. This he should maintain for an indefinite period, motionless. The poll remains the highest point. The horse champs the bit with closed mouth.

It is not absolutely necessary that the two hind legs be exactly parallel, the same as the two forelegs. On the other hand, that hind leg which is slightly to the rear must not be very far behind the point of hip.

To come to the full-halt out of the canter, needless to say, without any transitional strides, the same aids as mentioned above are to be applied, with the exception that corresponding to the almost invisible lateral bend of the horse's spine the outside rein must have slightly more resistance. The outside hand is effectively seconded by the bracing of the back and deepening of the seat bones, especially the inside seat bone, and further by the lengthened legs with very low heels.

Should the horse have an inclination to evade with its inside hind leg and dropping onto the outside shoulder, it is advisable to execute a slight shoulder-fore movement during the preparation for the halt.

The more impulsion the horse develops during the last canter strides, on constantly flexed yet shorter striding hocks the lighter the leg and rein aids can become; so that with well-schooled horses these aids can in the end be reduced to mere hints which take second place to the bracing of the back and subsequent slight shift of the rider's weight.

With increased fluency, suppleness and full acceptance of the aids, the full-halt can be achieved immediately from the walk; and from the collected trot and canter in one or two horse's lengths.

In the case of horses with weak hindquarters or weaker back muscles, the demands must be much less. It is advisable to ride such horses in a forward seat, low reins, asking for only a modest high carriage (see page 71).

Fault	*Correction*
Response to the command to the halt is too sudden and too jarring because of too heavy hand aids.	Lighter hand, predominant emphasis on lower back and leg.
The horse leans on the rein during and after the halt.	Upper body of the rider should be kept as vertical as possible. If the rider leans back this will only emphasize the tendency of the horse to lean on the reins.

Fault

The horse having been brought to a halt creeps backwards or sideways with his hind legs and evades to the left or right. He pulls against the rein, tosses his head or overbends.

The hind legs without being bent come too far forward at the halt and remain in this faulty position.

The front legs at the halt are behind the vertical.

One front leg at the halt is ahead of the vertical.

Correction

Having come to the halt, the hands should not remain in a pulling position, but should give. Even *before* the horse has been brought to a halt, the aids should have been more carefully applied. Raising of the neck should not be exaggerated!

Allow the forehand to move forward about one hoof's length.

Same as above.

Pick up with rein on the same side.

Standing square at the halt
Riding Master of the Cadre Noir.
Hind legs are under the point of the hip.
Complete, confident halt on the aids.

The halt and standing still
The author.

The halt and standing still

At the halt the hind legs are pushed too far forward and remain in this false and unbent position. The front legs are behind the vertical. False vertical bend of the neck. Poll is no longer the highest point. The horse's forehead is behind the vertical.

The halt and standing still
The halt has been achieved without legs and 'with hand brakes.'
There is no ideal harmony between the mount and his rider. They
both appear somewhat embarrassed. The main points of support of
the rider: the stirrup and the horse's mouth.

C 7
Turn on the Haunches

AS SOON as the young horse can execute the second position (see page 41) and is able to carry himself effortlessly during both the collected trot and the canter, and can come to a proper halt (see page 101), he is ready to commence the turn on the haunches. During this lesson in collection at either the walk, the trot or the canter, the front legs make a circle around the hind legs which stay on the spot but never cease to beat in the cadence of the particular gait. During the turn, the inside hind leg is the pivoting point, except at the canter. The pivoting leg lifts itself off the ground to return to the same spot or slightly to the front (see illustration page 113).

The turn on the haunches, or the half-pirouette, basically *must* come from forward movement. Even if the turn is preceded by a halt, the legs must start the forward movement before the aids for the turn take proper effect. If this is not done carefully, then the turn on the haunches becomes a stiff staggering sideways movement from all the pulling and hauling on the reins, and this makes it easy for the inside hindleg to take root in the ground. You will see this sideways staggering frequently in dressage and horsemanship tests, when the command 'turn on the haunches from the halt' is taken all too literally.

But not only is the gymnastic value of the turn on the haunches completely lost in such an execution, it will actually be detrimental. The responsiveness in everyday riding will be harmed because the standing horse when given the unmodified turning aid will, by falling on its shoulder, and boring a hole with its inside hind leg into the ground, soon seek its support on the rider's hand. The horse's suppleness, the whole object of this movement, will be lessened rather than augmented.

Purpose: Effortless control of the completely obedient and willing horse in a reduced area and at all gaits because of impulsion, collection and suppleness. By means of this complete control, one of the chief goals of the training and applied exercises is achieved. Hand in hand with the practising of this turn on the haunches exercise goes an increase of the flexion and carrying ability of the hocks.

Aids: *As an introductory exercise*, it is suggested to do a half volte and reverse and in a *travers*-like way at the walk and the collected trot, gradually making it smaller and smaller.

To execute the movement itself, the rider puts the horse to 'position' and then asks for almost *but not quite* a full-halt (a three-quarter-halt), which has as its aim the interruption of the forward movement of the horse so that the turn can be done with the hind legs stepping in place and the assuring of the requisite greater collection. Both reins lead the horse (which before the halt already has been put into 'position') toward the direction of the turn, step by step, around the hind legs which remain on the spot, in a quarter, or half, circle.

A minimal lateral bending of the spine having been established by the inside leg, immediately behind the girth and driving, keeps the movement fluid and the legs from being stuck to the ground, also brings the hindquarters up underneath the horse. The outside leg supports this forward drive, and also has the role, by being immediately behind the girth, to see to it that the hindquarters do not fall out. The rider having pushed his inside seat bone slightly forward and moved the outside shoulder forward in the direction of the turn, follows in the movement itself with lower back and leg aids that keep the horse gently and to the fore on the bit. The rein aids will be most effective when their influence is mainly in a straight line to the horse's mouth — the rider's elbows being close to his body — and lead through the rider's back to the horse's back. The complete harmony of the forward-sideways movement will have been achieved when during the turn the rider's driving aids result in the horse's more flexed hind legs moving a little further forward to carry the weight. Rein aids to the rear would have the effect that the spring action of the hindquarters would be suppressed and taken out of the turn.

With a horse in which the carrying ability of the hindquarters has not yet been developed to this degree, the rider allows the horse to move a little forward during the turn. The purpose is always the same — that the horse willingly accepts the increased weight on the hindquarters and that the horse willingly, responsively, and supple, accepts the aids and, with a lightened forehand following the reins, steps around a circle without pushing to the inside. The putting in position and the halt before the turn as well as the leading round of the forehand must each follow directly one after the other.

The turn having been performed correctly, the horse will be about a chest's width away from the original track. The turn having been completed, the movement and direction is changed and the previous gait immediately resumed (unless one intends to school for counter-exercises, see pages 43 and 98).

When the turn on the haunches is executed at the canter, this movement is known as a half or complete pirouette and is expected only of highly trained horses (Grand Prix or Haute École). The same aids are used as mentioned above. During a complete pirouette, the horse will, in the same rhythmic canter strides, turn in five or six strides with the *outside* hindleg more deeply flexed, which at the beginning of each stride of the series alone catches up and supports the entire weight.

During all these turns on the haunches the horse must be so put to the aids that the rider is able at any moment to change the rhythmic steps or canter strides of the turn fluently and without hesitation into a straight, forward movement.

A horse which is unable to execute a turn on the haunches at the walk or trot without resistance does not have the right to be called a 'schooled finished horse'.

TURN ON THE HAUNCHES AT THE WALK AND TROT

Fault	*Correction*
The strides during the turn are clumsy, hesitant and without expression. The horse is leaning on the bit with a dead mouth and uses it as support.	The rider, with strong self-discipline, must immediately interrupt this form of turning and resume an energetic straight and forward effort and motion, and good carriage; and re-awaken the inhibited or lazy horse, push it up to the bit and then recommence.
The horse moves back during the turn on the haunches.	Lighter contact. Rider must avoid pulling to the rear, and allow the horse to move more forward. Increase supporting leg and back aids.
The hindquarters fall away to the outside.	More outside leg which re-establishes the correct lateral bend around the inside leg.
The horse evades the bit on the outside, rushes with stiffened lower jaw onto the inside shoulder, in anticipation of the rider's aids.	Half-halts. Prevailing inside leg and outside rein aids. Picking up the inside rein (see page 15), so as to re-establish the flexion in the lower jaw.
The horse avoids the increased weight on the hindquarters by throwing himself onto the outside shoulder.	The preventative outside rein aid.
The horse resists the bringing under and flexing his haunches.	The collection must be achieved before the movement is asked for.
The horse comes to a standstill during the turn.	Lighter hand. Lessen the difficulty the horse encounters by trying to make a fluent turn remaining on the same spot with his hindlegs by allowing the horse to make a small circle in a travers posture.
The hindquarters make a small circle instead of remaining on the same spot.	This is not an error as long as the hind legs have not learned to carry fully the weight when flexing. It is only a small omission in suppleness which will disappear completely by itself in time with the correct sequence of gymnastic exercises (see above).

Fault

Because of overeagerness, the horse goes too much forward so that the hindquarters describe a small circle (see above) instead of staying on the spot.

The rider asks for too fast a turn by pulling on the inside rein; the flexibility of the hocks thereby is lost and the horse is thrown out of the turn.

The rider exaggerates the pressure of the inside rein without the complementary movement of the outside rein. As a result, the horse evades towards the inside with the whole neck in front of the withers, falling onto the outside shoulder and goes backwards with the inside hind leg.

Correction

Easy half-halts with the outside rein, being careful to maintain the lateral bend. For the time being, in no way try to force the horse to remain on the spot.

Follow with the inside hand! (See also 'Aids' page 108.)

Preventative and straightened outside rein. Vigilant inside leg.

TURN ON THE HAUNCHES AT THE CANTER

Fault

Over-eager horses will attempt during the pirouette to avoid the lateral spinal flexion of their body and put the weight onto the inside shoulder. (See page 110). They are ahead of the aids and lose, simultaneously with the lateral bend, the even, elegant cadence of the canter.

Correction

Should the preventative actions of the low inside leg just behind the girth and the taking up of the inside rein not be sufficient (see page 115) to prevent the horse from turning automatically on his own, the horse must be brought back to a walk by a half-halt chiefly on the inside leg and outside rein (as in coming out of the *travers*). The movement is thus transformed into and executed as the pirouette, a turn on the haunches at the walk. After completion of that turn, the canter will be taken up again very quietly.

Later on, the canter can be resumed after the half-halt while still in the turn.

Because the canter pirouette makes the highest demands on impulsion and the complete ability of the horse to carry himself on his hindquarters, it would be premature to go into this movement of the Haute École much further at this point. Suffice it to say that any errors appearing in this gait would be corrected in the same manner as those described at the walk and the trot.

Turn on the haunches
Pirouette to the right.
The author.

Turn on the haunches
 To the right.

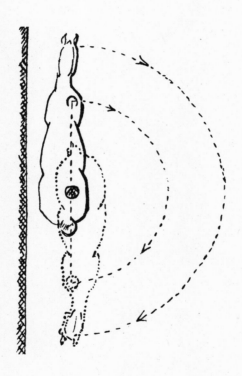

Two-track work

Shoulder-in left. I. Slight displacement, inside hind leg tracking on
outside foreleg. The so-called trotting position.

C 8
Two-Track Work

LET ME emphasize at the very beginning that two-track work can only be asked for in the second and third year's training of the horse and then only from a very few horses. A contrary point of view would ignore the fundamentals which are dependent on the horse's physique and temperament.

The teacher who, for reasons of his inexperience or false pride, does not respect the limits of the pupil entrusted to him, be that pupil two- or four-legged, is not a teacher and had better return to school himself.

This having been established, let me offer a brief characteristic which is common to all exercises on two tracks:

In the two-track work, the horse should move with a displacement of either the forehand or hindquarters — at the most one stride away from the track of the outside hindleg (shoulder-in) or, as the case may be, the outside foreleg (travers) — in a rhythmic, energetic and elastic movement sideways. During these movements, the lateral bend of the horse's spine should never exceed that which it would have were it executing a volte of six metres diameter.

The two-track movements are only a *means to an end* in dressage, either to enhance the education or to correct an error. Properly ridden, they will improve the general carriage, the impulsion of the strides, the straightness, the elegance, the swinging motion of the horse and improve the collection. *It must never be forgotten that the purity of the gait and forward impulsion are more important than the horse's posture and bending.*

All the exercises on two-tracks are asked for only because they enhance the ability of the hind legs to assume more and more of the weight, by transforming the energy of impulsion into weight carrying capacity. The lateral bend of the horse's spine required in two-track movements is equally essential in this transformation of power. They are therefore only a means to, and not an end.

The time to start the work on two-tracks commences during the second year of training — the first is the shoulder-in, the basis of all two-track movements — shoulder-in can commence when the horse is able to balance himself without losing his self-carriage and still remaining supple, also can go from an energetic medium trot to a collected one and remain confident and on the bit.

Purpose: The promotion of carriage and balance on a narrower basis of support, straightness and evenness, responsiveness and suppleness. Improvement of freedom of shoulder movement to the front and to the side. Perfection of the lateral spinal bend and therefore suppleness of movement as well as the obedience dependent upon this. Intensification of impulsion in the flexed haunches which can then project from collection to extension with more energy and elasticity. A means of correction for lack of straightness and lateral spinal flexion.

Aids: Never ask for work on two-track until the horse is in the correct 'position' and collection! Neither collection nor impulsion can be improved upon *during* work on two-tracks, and can never be created during work on two-track. During the exercise, see to it that there is purity of gait, that the horse's spine is flexed laterally, as well as a proper position of the neck in front of the withers. The inside aids should retain softness on the inside; the outside aids regulate the degree of the longitudinal bend and the displacement: all the aids see to it that the horse maintains his liveliness and animation.

Gaits: At a collected trot and collected canter. At a collected walk only after the horse has been thoroughly schooled in that gait. The collected walk has no gymnastic value because the movement at the walk does not create enough impulsion.

Regarding the seat during work on two-tracks, note my remarks on page 44. Observing the basic principle of following the motion of the horse, the rider must take care that his centre of gravity should always be directly over the horse's centre of gravity. He therefore naturally follows along in the direction of the two-track movement thanks to the natural tendency to lower to the inside, formed by the concave bend of the horse, without allowing his hip to drop.

The position of the rider's legs and hands during all these exercises on two-tracks will be very easy for the good rider to maintain because his hips are always parallel to the hips of the horse, and therefore his legs will naturally assume the correct position; and since his shoulders are always parallel to the shoulders of the horse, his hands will maintain the most effective and natural position.

Work on two-tracks must be done only for short periods, interspersed with energetic work at the medium trot and disciplined pure (single track) voltes. In order to maintain the straightness of the horse, there should also be full-halts, the horse standing motionless and in complete balance with his body in the position of the two-track movement just interrupted (see page 125).

Through lack of understanding or because the rider is obsessed with personal ambition and is so overcome with the success of his two-track work he must ensure that the horse is not urged, coerced or forced until he loses his purity of gait and impulsion: bear in mind the saying 'One should not push a good thing too far.'

(a) SHOULDER-IN

A German rule in work on two-tracks and, in particular, of the shoulder-in states: 'Shoulder-in is not only the foundation of the work on two-tracks, but properly ridden is an exercise which can be of the most benefit to the education of the rider and horse.'

Any comment on this classical definition would simply weaken it.

The development of the shoulder-in and the exercises leading up to this or the first position (see page 41) with which the horse is now thoroughly familiar can most easily be achieved out of the quarter turn in the first corner of the long side of the school.

In this exercise, the collected horse is positioned to the inside with his forehand no more than one stride away from the footprint of the outside hind foot. The horse now moves along the track, looking away from the direction of movement − contrary head position − with the forehand always a little ahead of the hindquarters in such a fashion that the inside feet occasionally go over and occasionally in front of the outside ones.

Purpose: See Purpose of work on two-tracks on page 116. Shoulder-in movement and the counter movement to shoulder-in are most useful in the correction of faults which are the result of crookedness in the horse (see page 16). These faults express themselves in insufficient lateral bending of the horse's spine.

Aids: They resemble to some extent the ones used to produce a shoulder-fore (see page 41), the difference being a higher degree of their effectiveness and the resulting education of the horse.

To develop the shoulder-in, the rider turns the horse, which has been collected and flexed as in preparation for the volte, away from the track coming out of the corner. A half-halt with the outside rein prevents the horse from continuing beyond the first step of the volte and requires the horse, supported by the inside leg, to stride forward and sideways. The inside rein is responsible for the correct head-position and prevents, when necessary, together with an alternating inside leg, the moving inwards of the hindquarters. The outside rein controls the degree of bending, brings the horse onto the predetermined track and supports the outside shoulder. The inside leg around which the horse's body is bent, is held slightly behind the girth has the duty to keep the lateral bend of the spine and, together with the outside leg, to encourage the hind legs into regular, lively steps. The third duty of the rider's inside leg, supported by the outside rein, is also to achieve the sideways movement of the horse. This aid is a rhythmic pressure in time with the lifting of the horse's inside hind leg, in harmony with the sideways and forwards movement (see page 14).

Rider's outside leg prevents the falling away of the hindquarters and supports at the same time the sideways forward movement in that it encourages the forward movement in the direction of the displacement. So this leg also has two duties to perform − that of supporting and that of driving-on. Correspondingly, the leg has first to be behind and then right on the girth (see page 44).

The ending of the shoulder-in occurs just before the corner by coming into the corner on a normal single track, in which, at the cessation of the lateral movement aids, the forehand automatically places itself in line with the hindquarters. The corners and short side of the arena are ridden in 'position' at a collected gait.

On the next long side, the horse is then 'put straight.' This is achieved by aligning the shoulders in front of the hindquarters (see page 17).

An exercise of shoulder-in on the circle is really not to be recommended. As long as the hindquarters are not sufficiently and surely engaged, underneath the horse, the danger exists that the rider is deceived, and the young horse places his hindquarters to the outside instead of the shoulder to the inside. The larger circle which the hindquarters must describe in the shoulder-in, misleads the horse into alleviating the burden of carrying himself with his hocks bent by leaving his hindlegs behind.

Coming to a halt: Principally, the outside aids must be used (see page 125).

Gaits in the Shoulder-In: Collected trot and canter. The latter chiefly for corrective purposes and then usually only in the shoulder-fore position, that is on normal single track.

Fault	*Correction*
Outside shoulder falls out, resulting from too strong use of inside rein; and therefore the neck, which has been pulled to the inside, becomes loose in front of the withers. This usually happens going to the right (crookedness).	Support with the outside rein while using a lighter inside rein. More definite driving forward of the horse's outside hind leg by the rider's outside leg slightly behind the girth.
In spite of drive-on aids and a light hand, during the shoulder-in and during other two-track movements, the horse does not seek the bit and comes behind it trying to hide behind	If the reason is of a careless resistant nature, the horse must now be ridden on single track in ground-covering strides and must be driven onto the bit. The correction will be most effective if he is ridden by an energetic rider in the

Fault

the bit.

During the shoulder-in, the horse goes into the wall.

During work on two-tracks, the horse loses expression and regular rhythm of the paces, becomes hurried or dragging.

In the exercise the shoulder-in to the right, many horses develop the habit of lowering their right ear and tilting their head to the left so as to avoid the pressure of the bit. This is an indication that the even contact with the rider's hand has been lost and the horse has made himself free of the outside rein.

Many horses try to delude their riders in the shoulder-in to the left in that they apparently yield willingly to the inside leg. This yielding is, however, nothing but an escape from the leg into crookedness with a straight spine.

The horse hurries and its steps become irregular.

Short, square horses with very round barrels or those with hay bellies resist the lateral bending of the spine.

The horse leans on the rein, stumbles and overreaches.

Correction

open straight forward and the horse is reminded that he is a forward moving animal.

In the direction of the position, turn to the inside of the track at more of a right angle.

Cease work on two-tracks and return to a strong tempo to rekindle the lost forward impulsion.

Re-establish evenness and straightness at a working trot as described on page 17. This is the best method of correcting this error, the most permanent and that which goes to the root of the problem. However, should there not be time to do this, for instance, during a test, then an immediate remedy would be to drive the horse straight aligning the fore and hind-quarters with driving leg aids and active placement of the horse's shoulders. It would never be advisable to try to re-establish the balance of the horse's head by heightening the hand on the side of the lower ear. To achieve the resumption of even contact, and correct lateral flexion of the neck, much sensitivity and practice is necessary with an unusual degree of ability to push the horse on. Should the rider lack these qualities it would only and inevitably result in the diminishing of the movement.

The rider's outside leg must take care of the lateral bend of the spine. The counter shoulder-in exercise, page 120, will be helpful.

Cease movement on two-tracks. Go back to normal track and establish the horse's carriage.

Make less demand. In horses with conformation problems, minimize work on two-tracks, do more turns on the forehand and leg yielding, as well as the useful substitution in such cases, increasing and decreasing the curve when riding into the corners.

Too much has been asked. Return to lateral bending exercises in the first and second position!

119

TEOH-5

Fault

The rider exaggerates the use of the inside rein. The resultant over-bending of the neck causes loosening at the withers and encourages the forcing-out of the shoulders. Long, thin-necked horses are especially susceptible to this.

Correction

Outside rein keeps the neck straight in front of the shoulders. Inside rein aid lighter. Energetic driving aids, particularly with the outside leg immediately behind the girth.

The rider attempts too early in the training of the horse to ride the corners at shoulder-in. Since the hind legs have a longer path to cover, it is a temptation for the horse to let his legs hang back thus avoiding carrying weight, fully engaging his hindquarters, avoiding the effect of the rider's lower back and so to *lose collection*.

Only ride the shoulder-in through the corner with such horses where the collection can be maintained and the hindquarters kept underneath him.

Rider applies his inside leg too far backwards. Therefore, its effect is only sideways and the lateral bend is lost.

Inside leg slightly behind the girth (see page 117).

(b) COUNTER SHOULDER-IN

Since this exercise complementary to the shoulder-in is a corrective one — for instance, if the horse is leaning or becoming loose in the withers or in the neck in front of the withers — it is then of great value and should therefore be discussed a little.

In order to go from the straight line to the counter shoulder-in, the rider places the horse first in 'counter position' (the exercise complementary to 'position') in order, on the one hand, to secure the bending of the side nearest the wall, now the *inside:** and, on the other hand, to be better able to limit the distance that the outside hind leg will move outwards at the next corner because of the sideward movement of the hindquarters toward the inside of the school at that point. The retention of the outside hind leg is all the more important because there is no supporting wall, thus making its escape easier.

We take only a slight displacement, so that there is only the width of one hoof toward the centre of the riding school. Now the newly placed inside hindleg follows the tracks of the outside foreleg. This is the so-called 'counter trot position' in which, as in the elementary work, the position for the trot widening the track of hoof prints and form three parallel lines (see also half-passes, page 127).

---

*It is always the *bend* that determines which side is the 'inside' or 'outside'.

Displacement, one stride maximum (80 centimetres).
Two-tracks
Shoulder-in to the right.

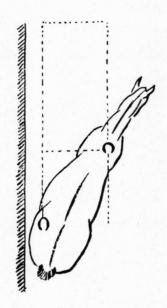

Two-tracks
Riding through a corner in right shoulder-in.

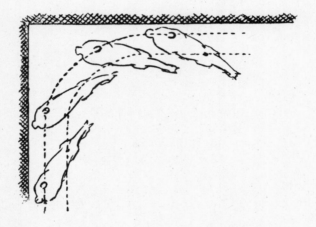

Seat and aids are the same as with the shoulder-in. The supple seat, adapted to the bend of the horse's spine with its unforced, natural inclination to the hollow side and the weight going with the sideway movement should be sufficient to maintain impulsion.

(c) TRAVERS

When during shoulder-in the rhythmic and lively gait is maintained in a collected self-carriage and a perfect lateral curve of the spine, then short periods of travers can be introduced. This movement is essentially closely related to the shoulder-in and should be developed out of this movement. However, outwardly there are some differences, and they are the following: During the travers, the hindquarters are directed to and positioned on the inner track. The outside legs step in front of and partially cross over the inside legs, so that the horse moves sideways and forward in the direction of the bend (looking in the direction of movement). The development of the travers comes from the second position, referred to as 'the position,' (see page 41) with which the horse by now is thoroughly familiar, that exercise having been part of the first exercises in lateral movements. It is best executed when coming out of the corner and changing through the diagonal of the whole or half school. In this way, the rider is able to maintain impulsion without being hemmed in by the wall. Once the horse is acquainted with this new lesson, the transition to travers can be executed elegantly and in an organised manner by allowing it to flow forward from the last stride of a true volte on a single track, since the horse in the volte already has the lateral bend necessary for travers (see page 135).

Purpose: See also under 'Purpose of Two-Track Movements' page 116. This exercise of the travers serves especially for the completion of the required collection and bend through the shoulder-in movement the increase of obedience to leg and rein aids, and the strengthening of muscles of the hindquarters. Furthermore, the travers guarantees a better control of the outside hind leg than the shoulder-in, since as in the shoulder-in it cannot voluntarily hold back but instead must step in front of and over the inner hind leg, which blocks the easier and more comfortable way.

Aids: They are similar to those which are used to put the horse in 'position' (see page 41), and differ from them only because of the stronger degree of effectiveness and resulting in the obvious and characteristic moulding of the horse.

The aids which put the horse into the travers position from a well-ridden volte, or a quarter volte on single track out of the corner, are the following:

Displacement, one stride maximum (80 centimetres).

Two-tracks

Travers.

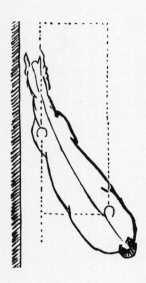

Two-tracks

Riding through the corner in travers.

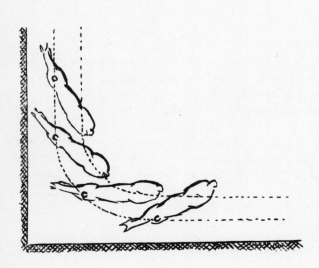

Inside rein maintains the head position and sees to the requisite bend; simultaneously it leads the horse.

Outside leg behind the girth initiates and maintains, together with the inside rein, the sideways movement.

The inside leg, around which the horse is evenly bent, slightly behind the girth, stimulates the lively forward movement and maintains a fluent and energetic forward progress. It also limits, when necessary, the degree of displacement of the hindquarters.

The outside rein, together with the outside leg, regulates the amount of bend and displacement and prevents the shoulder from falling out in that it holds the neck firmly in front of the withers. *The bend of the neck must always be in complete accord with the horse's spinal bend* — in other words, it must be 'true.'

The corners, in contrast with the shoulder-in, are ridden after a half-halt as a turn on the haunches in motion, the hind feet describe a smaller arc. It is therefore easier, in spite of the greater weight than in shoulder-in, to maintain the bend in the corners. It is essential that although the arc of the hindlegs be smaller and demand shorter strides, those strides keep the same rhythm as those of the forehand' turning on the larger outer arc.

As the travers movement demands more collection, and the striding of the outside legs from the stretched and lengthened side toward the hollow side demands considerably more strength, than the shoulder-in, these travers exercises should be alternated frequently with large and small voltes on a single track (see page 116), and in general be ridden only for a very brief intervals.

As in the shoulder-in, so in the travers, a flowing full-halt is the signal test that the balance of the horse and the resultant self carriage have been maintained (see page 116). Most important are the outside rein and the inside leg which prevent the horse's inside hindfoot evading to the inside or holding back.

The transition from the travers to the single track is achieved by adjusting the alignment of the forehand to the hindquarters.

Signal to halt: Chiefly with inside leg and outside rein.

Gaits at the Travers: Collected trot and canter, the latter only with totally straight, supple horses; otherwise there is great danger of the evasion of the inside hindleg. This crookedness creeps in especially frequently when cantering to the right.

Fault	Correction
Horse's neck is too bent in front of the withers (vertical false flexion). Vertical positio. is too high without	Increase the use of the inside leg and the outside rein; inside hand lighter.

Fault	*Correction*
lateral flexion of the spine and flexing the hindquarters.	
The horse resists the outside leg.	Change and execute counter shoulder-in. Frequently an increased use of the outside rein will be sufficient.
The horse with stiff back from neck to croup, is inclined to cross the outside hindfoot more to the side rather than to the front. Impulsion is lost and the hindquarters avoid the full weight and flexion.	The rider's inside leg must act preventatively and increase the forward drive. Presumably, the preparatory gymnastic exercise leading up to and including shoulder-in — which is the basis and foundation for all subsequent travers-like two-track movements — was not sufficiently thorough.

(d) THE RENVERS

The renvers is the counter-lesson to the travers. The footfalls of the forehand imprint the inside of the track, in such a fashion that the imprint of the outside front foot is at the most one stride sideways from the track of the inside hind foot, i.e. the one closest to the wall. The horse here too follows in the direction in which he is looking; however, he is turned, as in the counter-position, against his bend (see page 43). The riding of counter-position is thus a preparation for renvers. The development of the renvers should be executed in a fluent movement without hesitation. This is best achieved if the bend and the succession of hoof prints remain similar to those in the previous exercise, so that the renvers can be developed out of it by itself and unrestrained.

There are a number of transitions from travers to renvers (see also page 136): Change rein on the diagonal or short diagonal in travers and without altering position, upon reaching the far wall, continue in the renvers. Or without changing rein, go into renvers in the corner. Also effective is the turn on the hindquarters from the travers, when completed position the hindquarters in oblique direction to the wall, while the forehand stays the width of the chest away from the wall (see 109); then continue in renvers.

A helpful although indirect transition from the travers to the renvers which results in making the horse very attentive and sensitive is the following: From the first corner of the long side, at the travers, then upon reaching the centre of the long side, decrease the track, proceed two lengths straight ahead, then at first with shoulder-in and afterwards with renvers (change of bend and position of feet) move back to the track along the wall. It is essential that the rider allows time during the two lengths straight ahead to prepare the horse for the change of position and to maintain impulsion.

Purpose: The higher standard required for the turns in renvers make the horse more flexible and also makes the rider more skilled and effective.

Aids: They, as well as the seat, are the same as those for the travers. Only in riding through the corners must the rider — as in turns in 'counter position' — shortens the steps of the forehand, chiefly by the outside rein, which now becomes the leading rein, and, by moderating the position as well as driving-on with the inside leg, assure the maintaining of the rhythm and gait.

Faults	*Correction*
As in the travers. Particularly too much of a bend in front of the withers and falling away of the outside shoulder.	As in travers.

(e) THE HALF-PASS

The simplest and for the horse the easiest form of two-track work is the half-pass in which the displacement is only about the width of about one hoof, so that inside forefoot and outside hind foot track the same line. This is also called, somewhat improperly, the 'canter position' (compare with 'trot position', see page 120). As in the travers, the outside legs step in front of, but not over the inside legs. The head position and the bend are in the direction in which the horse is moving.

The reason why the half-pass is only mentioned after the travers has been discussed, is that it is a very difficult exercise to ride with its combinations, and its changing directions, flowing from one into the other.

Half-passes are diagonal displacements on two-tracks, thus on an enlarged track, at a collected walk (this only for schooling), trot and canter. The particular figures to be carried out in the half-pass are determined by the individual dressage tests.

In the half-pass, the horse moves with a less marked bend and less displacement in the direction in which he is going — namely, sideways and forward — in such a manner that he is almost parallel to the side of the arena. However, the horse's nose and the inside shoulder should always lead in the direction in which the horse is moving.

Purpose: Half-passes, alternating to the left and to the right, are the best test to find out whether the horse is equally balanced and flexible on both sides. Should a difference in the degree of lateral bend or position be noticed, then it is an indication that the horse is not sufficiently flexible and supple on one side. A further aim of the alternating half-pass is to achieve harmony of the aids in the changes of direction.

Two-tracks

Renvers to the left on the right hand. Forward and sideways
striding of the outside (right hand) pair of legs. The opening of the
rider's knee is wrong. The horse tilts his head. The right ear is lower
than the left ear.

Two-tracks

Renvers to the right on the left hand. As the result of the correct
bend which follows the whole length of the horse, the left rein lies
comfortably on the convex bulge of the neck.

Displacement, of one stride maximum (80 centimetres).
Two-tracks
Renvers.

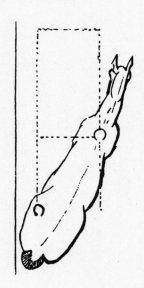

Two-tracks
Riding through a corner
at the renvers.

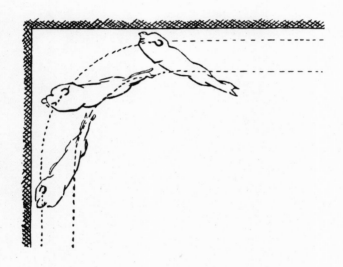

Two-tracks
Half-pass to the right (Lippizaner) No.1.

Two-tracks
Half-pass to the right (East Prussian) II.

Horse's inside (right) hind leg evades to the inside and does not follow sufficiently the forward line because the rider's inside (right) leg, around which the even lateral bend of the horse's spine should take place, is stretched away from the horse's side and therefore cannot fulfil its dual function of taking care of the bend and driving on. The rider is tense in his shoulder blades. As a result, his seat is forced.

Further, each and every correctly ridden half-pass, be it single or multiple, is an excellent means to increase the freedom of the shoulders in the forward and sideways movement, and, having been freed from the boring arena wall, to keep the horse moving with impulsion.

Aids: The first lesson of the half-pass commences, not quite halfway along the short side of the arena, at which point the rider turns his horse down the centre line of the school. The rider then collects his horse and places him correctly in position and rides approximately three more strides straight ahead. Then with the outside rein he performs a half-halt and half-passes towards the centre of the long wall — on the same rein — so that the forehand of the horse is always a little closer to it than the hindquarters when approaching the long wall. At the same time, the inside rein secures the correct head flexion. The rider's outside leg with low heel behind the girth, supported by the rein on the same side, keeps the horse moving 'sideways' by a sidewards pressure with each lifting of the horse's outside hind leg.

The inside leg, around which the horse is slightly bent, lays deeper, barely behind the girth, and 'rides forward', always ready to push a hesitating horse forward. The rider's inside leg also has the job of preventing the horse's hind legs from running ahead and is supported in this by the inside rein. Rider and teacher (the latter frequently controlling from in front of the horse) must be extremely careful to ensure that the horse does not tilt in its poll and neck, as well as taking care that the inside shoulder is set slightly forward and always leads in the direction in which the horse is going. Having now reached the long side of the school, on the track, the horse's position is re-established and it is ridden straight forward or put in the opposite half-pass movement to the centre of the short wall (double half-pass).

Eventually, the half-pass can also be made the second part of a half-volte and reverse, or be developed out of the shoulder-in on a straight line towards the centre of the school or arena by means of increasing the outside and lessening the inside leg aids.

In dressage tests when the more advanced half-pass is to be carried out to specific markers, it is just as much a fault not to reach the designated spot as to go beyond it. If the number of strides is specified, then it is also imperative that the rider counts correctly.

Once the half-pass has been achieved with lively, springly and weight-carrying haunches, so that the horse develops great impulsion and an even cadence, which gives the spectator a sensation of watching a work of art, then the goal has been reached.

Fault	*Correction*
The horse tries to evade and moves away from an even contact thus freeing itself from the reins.	Put the horse back on a single track.
The horse loses the expressive, gliding, cadence of its strides and drags on leaden feet which seem to be glued to the ground.	First establish and secure impulsion on a single track; then, by creating impulsion with the help of half-halts and changes of pace, bring the horse back into position and rhythm.
During a half-pass on the zigzag, unequal development of both sides becomes apparent.	Improve the suppleness of the horse.
The horse throws himself on his shoulders into the movement without waiting to be put into position.	This anticipating must be dealt with very vigorously. Using the inside spur could be more successful, in some instances, than the careful use of the reins, for the reins alone are unable to control this sidewards movement.
During the half-pass the horse does not respond to light aids for the halt. It does not remain quiet when standing in the direction of the movement. Does not go forward unhesitatingly.	Put the horse on the aids with more care, and hold between hands and legs.

(f) TRANSITIONS FROM ONE TWO-TRACK MOVEMENT TO ANOTHER

This has already been mentioned to some extent in the discussion of the individual movements. The purpose is to heighten the horse's attentiveness to the aids and to increase his suppleness — his readiness to obey and comply with each requirement — to the highest degree.

These transitions can be combined in various configurations. However, a rule in the riding and aesthetic sense is that they must be developed with presence and increasing free forward movement from the previous exercise. Turns on the forehand should now be avoided, because it encourages the hindquarters to carry less weight and collection is lost.

The most elegant and natural changes from one two-track exercise to another are when the position and the lateral bend of the spine remain the same, and only when the forward and cross stepping of the same set of legs is used.* In this, the rider can, at the same time as changing the two-track movement, achieve the exercising and working of alternate individual hind legs. However, through this work he does not achieve the increased carrying the flexing of the legs and haunches which can only be

---

*During the transition from the travers to the renvers by means of the turn of the haunches, the sequence of the footfalls remains unchanged.

achieved on a curved line, but nevertheless he can arrive at an increased suppling and command of the hind legs.

One such transition achieved merely by changing the sequence of footfalls is, as already described, the transition from shoulder-in to *travers*, which is achieved by riding through the corner, on a single track, in the bend of a shoulder-in, as a quarter-volte and subsequently continued as *travers* (see page 123 et seq.).

A further such transition is that from *travers* to the shoulder-in, in which the horse, after a simple volte developed out of a *travers*, is pushed by the rider's legs into shoulder-in while moving forward.

The same aids are also effective to achieve the shoulder-in after the horse, subsequent to a *travers*, has been moved straight forward, by the pressure of the rider's leg aids, following the line of the forelegs and maintaining the position, on normal single track.

Two-tracks

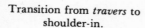

Transition from *travers* to
shoulder-in.

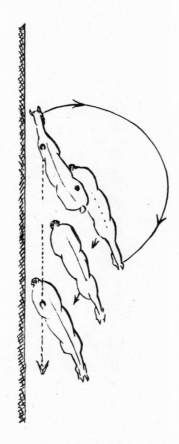

Transition from *travers*
to *renvers* is achieved
by means of the turn
on the haunches.

C 9
Simple and Flying Change of Leg
at the Canter

IN THE simple change of leg the horse must be brought back to a walk on a straight line (compare page 96). The change to the walk must happen directly from the canter (in other words, without trotting steps in between), easily, but surely. After two or three definite strides at the walk, during which the position of the horse has been re-established, the canter lead is resumed on the opposite leg. It is particularly important that the transition to the walk and the newly developed canter be achieved on the normal single track.

Aim of the simple change of leg is to make the horse more active. The more schooled the horse is, the sooner can he be put into a canter from a halt.

The fluent execution of a simple change is the essential prerequisite for flying changes,* which already falls into the domain of movements of High School.

According to the description of the flying change in the German Rule Book, this movement 'must be accomplished without interruption and without hesitation in a good forward canter movement and without the horse becoming crooked to one side or the other being thrown from one leg onto the other in the changes. The change must be accomplished with fore- and hindlegs at the same moment, and not in two movements with first fore- and then hindlegs. A thrusting upwards of the croup is wrong.'

The horse must be so trained that he obeys the aids given at the moment when the outside hind leg pushes off during that brief moment of suspension, in the air and to which he responds in a split second. If the horse's instant readiness to obey is lacking or if the horse anticipates the will of the rider, the flying changes so produced *will not be the result of*

---

*Flying change as described in the rules of the High School is not a basically difficult movement for the horse inasmuch as every foal has the inborn ability to change the lead when in the middle of a stride. The problem is more for the horse to respond to a schooling aid and instantly on command to break into the canter from a halt and the walk. When this is executed perfectly, it belongs to the most advanced movements of the High School.

co-ordination and harmony with the aids; and from an equestrian, aesthetic and artistic point of view such flying changes are worthless.

Purpose: To enhance the horse's gymnastic ability, across country, and in the arena.

Procedure to Teach Flying Changes: Before the rider can attempt flying changes, the horse must be able to make a perfect canter change directly from the walk with no transitional steps. Also, the horse must move into the desired canter without the slightest hesitation on the gentlest of aids, given by a bracing of the rider's lower back and inside leg in co-ordination with a slight intimation of the inside rein, with the support of outside leg. It is equally necessary that the transition from the collected canter to the walk be prompt, easy and precise, and achieved through the rider's back and inside leg.

The horse having been prepared as outlined above, and in order to make him understand what is expected of him, the logical teaching from the simple change to the more difficult movement in the flying change would be achieved by the following.

At the beginning of a lesson the horse has, as usual, first been ridden freely and then brought onto the aids, while moving in a supple gait, and he will now be taken to the top end of the school and put on a circle to the right which is so large that he will be effectively enclosed by the three walls. Take up a lively strong walk. At the centre of the short side, where the horse finds moral support in the wall, and where supporting and turning aids are minimal, the horse is repeatedly given the aids to break into a canter, always at exactly the same spot. At the completion of several strides, perhaps after a half circle, he is brought back to a strong walk. Upon reaching the short side again, renew the canter, and so on.

At every change to the canter, the rider uses exactly the same *aids*; he adds only a slight aid by means of his voice saying quietly 'Canter.' This exercise is continued until the physical aids, which should be reduced to slight indications until they are practically substituted by the voice.

The horse now having understood this exercise and being ready to execute the command on the slightest indication, the rider, after a fairly long interval of moving the horse at a free walk around the whole riding school, takes him to a spot removed from the centre of the short side where the horse performed the previous exercise, and puts him into the counter-canter, e.g., canter on the left lead going to the right. Now upon reaching the spot in the centre of the short side of the school where he previously always gave the aid to canter to the right, he will quietly and in a relaxed manner give the accustomed aids, including the voice command, for the right-lead canter. Should the horse not react to the aid, the rider must repeat it very quietly, without increasing his aids which would only result in a startled horse bolting.

It is probable that after the horse has made a few awkward attempts to try to obey this new command, he will be successful in finding the correct sequence to the right lead. The rider praises him, canters around the whole arena and then gives him a long rest. Should the horse not react, in spite of many attempts to give the aids for the right canter, he must never be punished, but the rider must return quickly to the walk and start all over again as described above — and never forget to praise the horse when he understands what is expected of him. (If the movement remains impossible for the horse, then it undoubtedly is due to lack of good preparation.)

For the first few times of this exercise of the flying change, the rider should not forget that a lightening of the horse's back by going more along with the movement will help the hind legs in their unusual task.

When, after several tentative attempts, the first change has been achieved correctly, it is a good idea to repeat it on the same circle and at the same place two or three times in order to impress on the horse the action of the change of legs.

However, each change should be followed by a lengthy rest at a walk, on a free rein, in order to give the horse an opportunity to think over the achievement and digest it mentally.

During the following lessons, the horse's understanding will be further strengthened. From the early uncertain and awkward attempts the flying change will become more and more even and crystallized. It goes without saying that alternating with this lesson to the right is the circle to the left and the flying change in that direction. Schematically described — in reality it will hardly be achieved without backsliding — the subsequent logical development of the lesson would be the following:

1 Once the flying change has been established from the counter-canter to the inside canter in the middle of the short wall in both directions, then

2 it will be produced anywhere on the circle.

3 After this exercise the horse will be ridden straight along the school and the flying change from the outside will be asked for. At the first effort the well-rounded corners can be used with advantage.

4 Then the flying change is attempted from the inside leg to the countercanter. For the time being, this is done at the centre of the long side so as to avoid the vicinity of the corners as must as possible. During this period of training, it is helpful to go along the outside wall which enables the rider to keep the horse straight on the countercanter. With the correct shoulder leading, an evading of the hindquarters can more easily be avoided (compare also page 99).

5 When the flying changes on the straight — from countercanter to canter and vice versa — proceed effortlessly and fluidly, one can go a step

further and practise these changes on a straight line away from the wall in the middle of the arena.

6 Finally, the flying changes are executed from the inside to the outside on fairly flat serpentines, initially with large diameter, when possible in a large manege in the open.

In order to accomplish a series of flying changes, with a specific number of strides in between, the rider must be quite clear how many canter strides are necessary before he can bring his horse back to a perfect walk without the horse losing his balance and without dropping his shoulder. Then he will also know the number of canter strides after which he can ask for a flying change without risking confusion.

For example: The horse which is confident in a single flying change and which is capable after five canter strides of coming back to a pure and relaxed walk, will, when asked, execute a second flying change in the sixth stride without much further ado.

The methodical rider will not ask for this second flying change on the sixth stride initially on a straight line, but at first on the circle from the outside to the inside canter, later on, on a straight line from the outside to the inside, and ultimately from the inside to the outside.

Flying changes every fifth stride are again conditioned by the ability of a horse to come back to a perfect walk at the end of four canter strides, and it goes without saying that the flying change every sixth stride first must be perfect. If one continues in this way it can be expected that there will not be too many difficulties in eventually achieving the flying change every other stride.

The teaching of the flying change at every stride, will not be discussed here, because the nature of the succession of movements in the canter stride, requires a system slightly different from that above.

Simple and flying change of lead
Flying change of lead from right to left.
The new inside foreleg must virtually fly out of the shoulder easily
with an energetic movement.

Extended trot I

The horse's outline should improve and become larger than in the medium trot; the horse should stretch out of himself; the rider should have the feeling of riding uphill, glued to the saddle. The energetic push of the lowered hindquarters encourages the powerful, longer stride. The somewhat heavy neck of the horse could be stretched a little more.

C 10
The Extended Trot

WHILE THE collected trot improves the carriage and posture of the horse which is moving with impulsion, elegantly and fluidly — but not with a long reach — the purpose of the extended trot, is an intensification of the medium trot, from which it is developed, especially in increasing the engagement, and energetic action of the hind legs. The forehand comes high out of the shoulder. One must be able to differentiate quite clearly between the bending, stretching and position of the legs. However, the resulting movement, must in no way increase the tempo above that of the medium trot. In comparison to the medium trot, the horse should now be carrying himself correctly with his face slightly further in front of the vertical and in spite of less collection, always with a lively mouth, the neck stretching through the poll to the bit without leaning on it, and without becoming unbalanced, and without increasing his speed with the slight stretching of the neck.

The extended trot must only be the natural succession of the maximum impulsion and derive from the hocks. Thereby the extended trot is the proof of the degree of our success in improving the carriage and impulsion of the horse.

A cramped stretching of the forelegs and shoulders which is only an apparent extension of the forehand will toss the rider about and will fulfil neither the purpose nor the intention of the movement. The extended trot, strictly a dressage gait such as the collected and extended walk, is a combination of the entire gymnastic training of the horse and, just as with those two gaits, should not be asked for before the end of the second year of training, and then only with horses of considerable talent.

Purpose: Perfection of the medium and collected trot, for which, as for the two-track movements, it sharpens the impulsion and exuberance. It develops, as does the extended canter, the thrust of impulsion to the degree where it is limited only by the horse's conformation and temperament. It serves as a test and mirror for the degree to which we have been successful in developing the impulsion, the driving force and the carriage of the horse.

Aids: The extended trot is developed from a canter movement or from a medium trot, and is only ridden through the diagonal or on the long side of the school. When developed through the medium trot, the rider's legs drive the horse more definitely forward, without kicking. In order to achieve a transition that is fluent and without loss of regular cadence, the strides must be developed in harmony with the aids and only very gradually. The hand, guiding from a lower position and taking a more definite contact, allows the strides to become longer. The more free the tempo is, the more the rider must go along with the motion, controlling the horse with his lower back and seat. Despite less collection, the horse must be supple in the poll and always be ready to champ the bit.

During the correct extended trot, the rider remains easily and without effort in the saddle. The oscillating, shock-absorbing back draws him close from back to front in the movement and at the same time into the saddle. The rider has a feeling of *riding uphill* and no difficulty in sitting to the powerful, yet even and elastic, oscillating movements of the back which keep him deep in the saddle.

If the preparation has been too hasty and if the back is not pliant enough, then we must — which would profane a classic performance, yet nevertheless is given the official blessing by the FEI — resort to a rising trot. Therefore, a rider should aim to show his horse in the extended trot by sitting deeply and easily in the saddle so as to prove the preparation for this movement has been correct.

This ought not in itself to be taken as a criticism of the rising trot as such when used appropriately. It has become an indispensable exercise in the schooling of the horse. Its influence on the not yet supple horse is well known. But even beyond that we also use it most successfully with horses which are sluggish, which are extra sensitive in their backs or hindquarters, or which have for some reason become sour, in order to achieve an enthusiastic engagement of the hindquarters with a better disposition for the gait, and in general to make them happier to move freely forward.

Faults	*Correction*
Tense strides.	With lively working trot and energetic canter intervals, re-establish the suppleness of the horse and the liveliness of the gait.
Rushing strides. Frequently a sign that the aids have been given too drastically and too soon and have disturbed the rhythm.	Return to the medium trot. Then again very gradually ask for more, after the rhythm has been secured.
The horse forges and falls apart.	Shorten the tempo, improve the carriage. If the horse appears tired, do not ask for so much.
The horse leans on the bit. Despite the pushing of the hind legs, they do not come underneath the horse the way	Frequent transitions between extended and medium trots. During the required necessary half-halts, the horse must yield more to the

Faults

Correction

they should and do not flex during the forward movement. The weight is being driven onto the forehand.

pressure of the bit, and become more responsive to the reins by suppling his poll, so that the hindquarters are thereby caused to take more of the weight.

The hind legs spread and, as frequently seen in trotting-race horses, track to the outside of beyond the front feet. By this paddling movement, evading to the right and left, they avoid carrying the weight.

Cure of the symptom: Hold the reins further apart. Through schooling correction: Lateral bending work.

The front legs become tense and stretch in a jerky manner. They come down on a point behind that to which the toe is pointed at its highest elevation (compare page 61, medium trot).

The tense strides attest to the fact that there is not enough collection or suppleness. Symptomatic cure: Less rein effect. Lasting cure: Submission, suppleness and collection must be improved.

The line of the horse's face is behind the vertical.

By means of frequent changes between working and medium canter on a large circle, position the horse's nose to the front of the vertical. Light and low hands.

The horse very grudgingly accepts only that amount of contact which is absolutely necessary for a perfect extended trot.

Wait patiently, until the horse finds for himself that a more definite contact is necessary and then seeks it.

Horse becomes crooked.

At the beginning, a slight natural crookedness may be tolerated so as not to lose the rhythm or enthusiasm when the horse is being straightened up. The rhythm and forward movement are more important *for the time being* than the pure straightness. Resistances to one side in the poll and hindquarters which cause this crookedness should be corrected by the appropriate exercises, but never during the extended trot.

Rider is behind the movement.

The upper body of the rider should be more vertical. Low close knee. If necessary, to find his correct position, the rider should grasp the pommel.

The rider holds on to the reins too strongly, pulling back. His legs fall back.

Run the hand up the mane. Lighter hands. Legs slightly behind the girth and keep them there.

For the benefit of the all too ambitious young rider, I should like to add to this by no means complete list of errors, the comment that even the cleverest riding cannot give to some horses that free, yet at the same time elegant movement which other horses have by nature.

Extended trot II

The gait has been increased but along the lines of false tension. The strides are stabbing, with a stiff back, and the neck pulled backward, which should be allowed to stretch more.

Because of the incorrect carriage and the forcing of the trot, it becomes impure, (the left hind foot leaves the ground before the right forefoot, both of which should move simultaneously), that is, the hind is uneven in the sequence.

The stiff, unyielding back does not oscillate, the harmony between the forehand and hindquarters is lost. A horse only using its legs instead of his whole body.

Extended trot III

As contrast to the extended trot, the 'ground-covering' racing trot.
Notice wide and backward stretching action of the hindlegs, which
strike off later than in the classic trot, and which is forbidden in
that gait. (The world's champion trotter of all time — Greyhound,
1·55 1/4 min.)

C 11
The extended canter

IN THE same way that the extended trot is a development of the medium trot, so the extended canter results from the development of the medium canter (see page 66). It is derived by gradually increasing demands, when necessary by energetic driving aids.

Lengthening of the outline of the horse should, just as in the extended trot, come out of a slight extension of the neck and head while retaining the rhythm of the shorter canter. Strides of the horse become longer and lower as a result of the strong driving aids and the stretching forward and downward of the neck, the contact on the bit becoming more definite. The rider follows in harmony with the increased tempo, without falling forward, to avoid any interference with the horse's back and the movement of the horse.

The long easy canter strides makes the horse 'gallop into his neck and onto the bit' throughout the length of the horse's back. Nevertheless, he must always be in the hand of the rider, always be easily controlled. This is only possible if despite strong contact he remains submissive.

Just as the extended trot, so the extended canter is always ridden on a straight line. Not even the long sides of a 60 metres riding school or arena are sufficient to develop fully a good extended canter.

In the event that an extended canter is practised on a large rectangle, the shallow corners and short sides should be ridden in the medium canter. The suppleness and submission with which the horse responds to the half-halts necessitated by the corners are a good proof of his balance.

For full-halts out of the extended canter, the comments in previous paragraphs are relevant.

Purpose: A schooling and general purpose gait. Develops propulsion and thrust to their maximum. Serves as a hall-mark for submission, carriage and obedience at even the fastest tempo. A genuinely well-schooled horse should be able even in the extended canter to be ridden with one hand at any time and 'be able to be held with the seat.' Proof of this are those niceties, such as running your hand up the mane, letting the horse extend his neck champing the bit, and lengthening of the stride while on the bit.

An excellent way to awaken the heart and the enthusiasm of a dull, lazy horse.

As a working gait, ridden somewhat more freely, the extended canter is the daily bread for the hunter, the show jumper and, along with the free walk, the chief gait of the cross-country rider.

These brief words about the purpose of the extended canter will be augmented by a few comments. They are, however, only applicable to the action and capability of average horses. We should note briefly that there are individual cases where the rider should and must exceed what might appear to be limitations without danger to the horse's carriage and joints. With especially suitable horses, development of the natural gaits should not be suppressed by thoughtless adherence to a schedule appropriate to the average horse.

The extended trot, which is only a schooling and not a working gait, must not be used in cross-country. Should a rider wish to increase his speed from the ordinary trot (275 metres per minute — same as working trot), he then uses the medium canter (350 metres per minute) and a lengthened canter (400-500 metres per minute). The natural extension of this last canter then becomes the extended canter. It is possible, with a more free way of going than would be used for a schooling purpose, that this latter, on good ground, can be extended to 700 and even more metres per minute.

As regards aids and faults, as well as corrections, please refer to the chapter on medium canter, page 67.

C 12
Work at the Walk III
(a) THE COLLECTED WALK

ACCORDING TO the proven rule, 'The trot prepares for the canter, and the two of them prepare for the walk,' we shall only now, at the end of the second year's training, begin with the real work at the walk, the collection of the medium walk (see page 68) practised heretofore.

The collected walk as well as the extended trot are pure schooling exercises and just as the extended canter and the extended walk they are definite proof, guarantee and end result of the entire previous gymnastic training of the horse. This gait, with its high action carried by the flexed hocks, its elegant and fluid cadence and its confident and easy contact, belongs in the realm of the High School, in the same way as do the extended canter, extended trot and extended walk in their perfection.

With the correct harmony of gentle driving aids and even more discreet resisting aids, the collected walk would be achieved as follows. A high carriage appropriate to collection. The forehead vertical or slightly ahead of the vertical. The hind legs in the same rhythm as in other degrees of the walk, lively and flexed, are placed somewhat behind the imprints of the forefeet. The rhythm remains the pure four beat of the walk, but the individual steps, owing to the higher hock action, become more elegant. The horse maintains a definite but giving and absorbent contact, must always be ready to extend himself or take up a gait which covers more ground.

The collected walk should only be attempted at the end of the second year of education and then only for very short intervals.

Purpose: To heighten the readiness and hardiness of the horse in all directions.

Aids: To achieve collection at the walk is one of the most difficult exercises for the rider. It is for that reason that we frequently see the allegedly perfectly ridden and highly marked horse in dressage tests committing the worst faults at the walk.

The work preparatory to the collected walk — starting with a free walk on a loose rein, and later on a long rein, working up to a medium walk — has already been described on page 68.

In the course of subsequent work, the collected walk is developed out of the medium walk or the halt. The manner of the development of the aids to achieve the collected walk is comprised in the following discussion of the most frequent faults and deficiencies.

Faults

The collected walk *is* insufficient because it is being asked of a horse which is not yet fully supple in his back or joints. Or, it *becomes insufficient* during a period of work because the horse has been ridden too long in collection and has not been given the opportunity to stretch from time to time and rest.

Over-eager horses try to free themselves from the rider's legs.

Often because of restlessness strong, nervous horses will adopt short, hasty and impure strides; they are yielding and see-saw themselves free from the reins.

The horse does not yield, not because of nervousness as described above, but because of laziness.

The rider exaggerates the alternating driving aids or drums the horse constantly and simultaneously with both legs.
The simultaneous hammering of the legs disturbs the rhythm of the gait. Further, with such continuous pommelling the horse will become insensitive and dead to the rider's legs.

Correction

Obvious in the description of the faults.

The rider's legs remain quietly and gently on the horse: this is the best way to calm the horse. Soon the rider will feel a more relaxed and obvious four-beat measure against his legs. The horse should respect the leg aids, but must not be afraid of them or flee from them.

First of all, with a quiet clinging leg (see above), calm the horse.
When the even four beat has been re-established, preferably without half-halts, if at all possible — the latter would only result in heightening the nervousness — the driving leg of the rider can now gradually and gently be applied sufficiently to achieve a more lively gait, without attacking the horse which is only too ready to tense himself anew in response to kicking aids.
As a result of being driven forward gently in a four beat stride, the horse will now be induced to accept an even and soft contact with more confidence than before.

The rider now actively uses his legs alternatingly in rhythm with the horse's movements, — possibly even in conjunction with the whip directly behind the leg — to stimulate more lively strides.

Should an alternating driving stimulation not suffice, then a short single or multiple energetic application of the spurs on both sides, together with an application of the whip, should make the horse more attentive to the more mild leg aids.

152

Faults

Correction

Besides, such driving aids only result in the stiffening of the hindquarters and the back, which breaks up the harmony between the hindquarters and forehand and results in the horse starting to pace or jog.

The rider exaggerates the restraining aids in the attempt to collect the horse into his hands. He allows, generally unknowingly, the reins (which in the walk would find the least resistance) to dominate,* and operates from the front to the rear rather than the opposite, from the rear to the front. The result is hindquarters stiffening themselves against the pressure of the reins and the loss of a rhythmic, expressive cadence.

The rider must watch his hand aids with strict self-discipline. They must never interfere with the movement of the horse and the bringing under of his hindquarters. Therefore a passive hand, which waits for the hindquarters brought and delivered to them by the rider's back.

The rider demands too soon in this work at the collected-walk a lively rhythm of the sort which can only be maintained with a horse that is fully schooled, completely supple in his hocks and has a stately carriage. The beginner or young horse is not yet equal to this dual assignment of being both lively and elegant; his strides become hasty and fragmented instead of focussed and diligent, or they can stiffen into a pacing-like sequence.

Strides must above all remain even and definite. The liveliness of the strides is secondary. This will result from a gradual heightening and strengthening of the hindquarters and be a natural result of the rhythmic driving aids.

(b) THE EXTENDED WALK

JUST AS the collected walk, the extended trot and the extended canter are the result of the whole previous schooling and gymnastic exercises of the education, so is the extended walk. It is developed out of the collected walk with the augmentation of the bending of the hindquarters and the hind-hocks which must result in increased stretching ability of the hindlegs.

As a perfection of the three-walks the extended walk can only be the result at least after two years' education of complete control. Hurried walking is far from being energetic walking, and even less a long stride. Long striding must come from the hindquarters and can only correctly

---

*When the hand is dominant, the rider has lost the war before the battle has begun.

express itself in the fore. Thanks to well tempered aids, the horse's back, neck and poll interact. The eternal fluttering of the reins has never produced a correct extended walk. With the correct preparation and effects, we see the extended walk as it is described both by the German LPO and the rules of the FEI. 'The horse goes with wide ground-covering strides that must be as long as is permitted by his conformation. Without hastening and impurity of the strides. The hind hoofprints reach far over the front hoofprints. The rider allows the horse complete neck freedom, without losing the contact or the feel of the horse's mouth (on a long rein) allowing him immediately the possibility of changing the gait or changing the direction. Middle and extended walk can also be ridden with the reins thrown away (the loose rein without contact with the horse's mouth).' The horse should go in natural carriage freely without resistance, the tail swinging in cadence with the horse's movement; with his neck stretched to the fore, nose extended, he is seeking the bit. He must follow the bit 'courir après le mors' as the Frenchman, Ecuyer Saint Phalle, very literally describes it.

Purpose: The deportment of the horse in the transition to the extended walk will give a clear picture whether the previous work during collection has been achieved without forcing. In this regard, the extended walk of the dressage test has the same aim as the concluding jump.

Furthermore, a demonstration of the long extended walk is the proof that the horse in spite of its utmost stretching and utmost reaching has maintained control of his body and has maintained his balance without having to rush.

Aids: For the development of the extended walk from the middle walk or the collected walk, the rider avails himself of the same drive-on aids as for the exercise 'lengthened strides on the rein', the only difference being that the hand does not follow, that the fingers opening allow the reins to go to the utmost of the horse's stretching neck down to the neck.

Error	Correction
During the transition to the extended walk, the horse pulls the rein with stiffened poll and tossing head out of the rider's hand, instead of seeking the hand with feeling lips and chewing and stretching of the neck naturally.	The previous work at collection has been forced. The back never gave in. Joints and muscles are not loose. The horse revenges itself as soon as it feels a freeing of the reins. Correction: commence by loosening and relaxing the horse, then achieve proper collection; and only after this proper collection, again ask for extended walk.

Error	Correction
The briskness of the hitherto ground-covering strides becomes hasty. The steps are short and hasty. The tail, instead of swinging in cadence with the gait, becomes stiff. Facial expression and ears look tortured.	Softer leg aids, not abrupt.

The collected walk and riding on the curb
'Caesar' by Anblick XX — Adlatus XX.

Extended walk
On a long rein to be noticed the excessive reach of the hind legs.

PART TWO

THE CURB

Use of the curb bit to complete the work of the snaffle,
to assure the correct of the horse
His submission, straightness and carriage

TOWARDS THE end of his second year of training when the young horse has developed to the point at which he is ready to collect himself in accordance with his physical development, the time has come to introduce him to the curb and to accustom him to its action and aids.

However, this is not to say that the horse from now on must constantly be ridden in a double-bridle! Getting the horse used to being ridden on the curb also serves the purpose of giving the trainer and the rider illuminating hints for what purpose and how correctional work on the snaffle can be used. Many deficiencies in the way the horse carries himself, how he moves, and how he accepts the bit become more perceptible, more visible, and more pronounced when the horse is being ridden on the curb.

The inexperienced rider, who up to now has measured the ability of his horse against the standard of his own illusions can experience all sorts of surprises when riding on the curb.

The person who, because of this bitter recognition, comes to the conclusion that further work on the snaffle is indicated (and in so concluding, will not be in bad company!), will have to say to himself that this follow-up work is possible* and can only be successful because of the action of the jointed (or broken) snaffle.

This is because (theory again!) with the snaffle the pressure exerted by the hands upon the mouth is felt in direct ratio, and the rider therefore is in a better situation to control the effect of his hands than he would be with the lever action of the curb. Besides, because of the way it is fitted, the curb being a solid bar does not allow a one-sided pressure.

Final choice of the suitable curb bit. The horse owner will presumably content himself with the more or less rich selection of curb bits among those at his disposal in the tack room, and chose the one least unsuitable to the dimensions of his horse's mouth.

We may hope that by his general equestrian ability, he will be able to make up for any possible insufficiencies and shortcomings as far as the correct measurements of the curb is concerned. Because as important as it is, that each horse be bitted with a curb fitting as close as possible and that it be adjusted so that it functions correctly, it may be pointed out that its perfect effect depends not so much on the *shape and fit of the curb bit* as on the *development and conformation of the horse* which has been built upon the previous thorough going work on the snaffle and prepared him for the acceptance of the curb effect.

---

*Since in my foreword I expressed the desire to refrain in this book from theorizing (whether successfully or not, the reader can now judge for himself), may it here be said that the discussion of the technical side of riding on the curb has been curtailed in further brevity as have other explanation of the 'why.'

The young reader eager for knowledge — for he still exists! — shall be made aware that in my books, 'Von der Koppel bis zur Kapriole' (From the Pasture to the Capriole) and 'Reitlehre von Heute' (Riding Instruction Today), he will find the full answers to his 'why's.'

At this point, somebody could well ask, why all this complication of curb bits? and cast serious doubts on the need for and purpose of the curb. He shall be answered both from the point of view of the academician as well as from the point of view of the practical rider.

Purpose: No matter how submissive the horse has become by the prior work on the snaffle, the *ultimate in impulsion* will be given only when he is ridden on the curb.

Forces of resistance, which with even the most submissive horse will occasionally momentarily be effective against the simple snaffle as he wastes his energy defending himself against it, can no longer come to fruition with the more consistent control of the curb bit. Instead this force with the more cushioned contact, is expressed and transformed into a positive energy, the horse moving with an elastic oscillating back through the poll, obedient to the rider's will, free moving, elastic strides with a sure elegant way of going. Especially when riding with a dropped snaffle rein, will our rein aids become refined — one thinks at this point of Colonel Podhajsky — and a consistent elastic contact between hand and horse's mouth is established as is only possible by the lever characteristics of the curb.

A further reason for using a curb, because of its stronger action and effect, is, without question, better control of the horse when riding in the open.

And, finally, to make a virtue of necessity, as commented at the beginning, a premature bitting with the curb will fulfil a purpose indirectly in that it will exaggerate errors in gait and contact which otherwise might have escaped the trainer's notice.

Then, as subtly and perfectly the movement of a horse that has matured to fully accept the curb will be influenced by the mouthpiece which prevents stiffening originating in the lower jaw to materialize, so short-comings in movement and the acceptance of the bit will be emphasized with a horse that has too soon been blessed with the curb. It gives us very clear indications of how to approach the unavoidable correcting work on the snaffle.

Preparation and aids for initial work on the curb: First of all it is primarily a matter of accustoming the young horse to this new bit and getting him to accept it confidently. This is best accomplished at medium gaits and on long lines in the open. In these ground covering rhythms, we get the horse to stretch and very gradually, with complete lack of restraint, to come into contact with the curb which has been completely inoperative and for the moment has no curb chain, or only a very loosely fitted chain.

After the horse has gained confidence and, after lengthy trotting periods with his face ahead of the vertical, has taken hold of the curb bit, all four reins can be gathered together in one hand, and the contact can be regulated by the free hand in such a way that the snaffle rein predominates.

For the moment all rein aids are initiated with the snaffle. In a turn, the outside curb rein is for the time being a little more relaxed, and is only gradually brought into effect after the horse had learned to yield to the pressure of the curb bit on the outside bar. It is usually in turning to the right that the left curb rein pinches and makes it difficult for the horse to execute the change in direction. The cause of this is too little releasing of the left and insufficient shortening of the right (inside) curb reins. In giving the aids, it is also proper that the rider, at each change of direction, regularly rearrange his reins — and without being asked or reminded.

When riding *on the curb with engaged snaffle*, the halts, as well as the above-discussed turns, proceed in general accordance with the same principles as when the snaffle alone is employed.

If you carry the reins in the *left hand*, the rider turns as with 'snaffle rein crossed over in the left hand' (right snaffle rein between thumb and forefinger in the left). To turn to the left, the left forearm and the left hand are rotated without altering the position of the upper arm from the elbow joint to the left to the degree that the back of the hand is turned down, the palm of the hand turned up.

To turn to the right, the opposite action takes place. In the 'falling over,' or the 'covering over,' as this otherwise faulty hand position is called, the back of the hand becomes turned upward and the palm of the hand downward.

In all turns to the right, should it be with both hands operating the snaffle or with the left hand alone leading, one must be aware that the left hand can, if necessary, be supported by the intervention of the second and middle fingers on the right (inside) curb rein. Otherwise it might happen, as previously mentioned, that the horse is guided by the right snaffle rein alone to the detriment of equal contact in the turn.

To avoid *pulling* and onesidedness in the rider, it is recommended that at times *the right hand alone* should do the leading. The aids are the same except that the 2.5 centimetre longer length of the left curb rein must be taken into consideration.

When after several unconstrained rides in the open, freedom of stiffnesses will be achieved by a lively forward movement and by accepting the rider's passive hand, the time has come to adjust the curb chain so that it creates the correct lever effect; and now in the riding school the whole process of development, as we started in the beginning, with relaxation and putting the horse onto the aids as previously described in this book, is begun again but now in unrestrained position. One should set aside several weeks for this. Shortening of the gaits as far as possible should be avoided. One must be ever mindful that the stronger bitting may cause or help a false bend at the neck and a lowering of the poll in many horses, and also getting behind the bit.

A complete and highly expressed collection is only requested when the horse is confidently and securely on the bit. For jumping and in difficult terrain, lengthening of the curb rein to eliminate its influence and effect is indicated.

Most of the errors which occur when riding on the curb originate from too hasty introduction of the horse to the curb, which causes him to frightened of it.

Faults	*Correction*
Horse tries to evade straightness by bending his neck sideways and thereby cancels the effect of the curb on that side.	The even contact can be re-established only *on* and *through* the corresponding snaffle aids (page 85, 'To Put To The Aids.'), since the curb with its solid (unjointed) mouthpiece cannot exercise a purely onesided influence.

The horse opposes the lever influence of the curb by (A) passive or (B) active resistance.

(A) The lower jaw evades backwards or sideways in that the horse further loosens his neck by stiffening the poll and comes behind the bit. The main points of this *passive resistance* are the stiff and *dragging* succession of the hindquarters as well as the back action no longer moving into and through the neck.

There is a further form of passive resistance particularly where the curb mouthpiece has not been carefully fitted and interferes with the freedom of the tongue. The horse will complete the evasion by elevating his tongue over the bit and pushing it sideways out of the mouth.

(B) The horse will turn to an *active form of resistance* because of an uneven, too strong pressure of the wrongly chosen, wrongly fitted curb bit and chain which afflict him with pain.

The previous, incorrect coming behind the bit now develops into a leaning onto the rein downwards or u pwards, supported by a stiff neck, the hindquarters dragging, *leaning against* the lever influence of the bit.

The willingness of the forward movement into the rider's hand achieved by work on the snaffle, as well as the elegant and supple neck, disappear in a flash and thus the control of *the hindquarters and all obedience*.

Conscientious follow-up work on the snaffle with the purpose of putting the horse securely on the aids. Should work on the curb nevertheless be continued, then the posture gained by the previous work will progressively be lost. Cause: as soon as the hind feet no longer step smoothly and fluidly forward reaching under the centre of gravity, but (a) either *drag to the rear* without impulsion, (b) or remain behind *braced* against the lever influence, the inadequately supported forehand carried too much weight and prevents the free striding, balanced position because of a hampered, inexpressive gait, weight on the shoulder and *loss of gait*.

To try to prevent the horse putting his tongue over the bit by tightening the nose band is a poor, and even worse, senseless and unimaginative way of correcting his symptom. The nose band must be so adjusted as to allow the horse sufficient space to rearrange his tongue in the tongue groove without difficulty.

Success will also be achieved if the rider through using his back and energetic leg aids, together with light rein aids is able to push the horse once more onto the bit, and encourage him to champ whereupon the tongue will push away from the jaw and resume its place in the tongue grove.

But these simple, pure methods, the tongue over the bit problem is reduced: 'as long as the horse is champing, he cannot misuse his tongue.' To be sure, a small measure of riding ability is needed to achieve this.

With this chapter I finally complete 'The Essence of Horsemanship' with suggestions in words and pictures; and wish you all 'the best possible riding conditions.'

Final illustration I
The piaffe the essence of the High School (Haute École).
These illustrations of the classic piaffe and passage added at the end of this book might serve as a little foretaste of the higher riding art as described in my books, 'From the Pasture to the Capriole' (Von der Koppel bis zur Kapriole), 'Riding Instruction Today' (Reitlehre von Heute), 'In the Saddle I Didn't Count the Hours' (Im Sattel zählt ich keine Zeit), 'Women, Horses and Books' (Frauen, Pferde, Bücher), 'Olympic Equestrian Competition, Paris, 1924' (Die Olympischen Reiterkämpfe in Paris 1924), and 'Masters of the Equestrian Art and Their Ways' (Die Meister der Reitkunst und ihre Wege.)

Final illustration II
Passage